W9-BEZ-500

WALTER DEAN MYERS

A Biography of an Award-Winning Urban Fiction Author

by Denise M. Jordan

Enslow Publishers, Inc.
40 Industrial Road
Box 398
Berkeley Heights, NJ 07922
USA
http://www.enslow.com

Copyright © 2013 by Denise M. Jordan

Original edition published as *Walter Dean Myers: Writer for Real Teens* in 1999.

Library of Congress Cataloging-in-Publication Data

Jordan, Denise.
Walter Dean Myers : a biography of an award-winning urban fiction author / Denise M. Jordan.
p. cm. — (African-American icons)
Includes bibliographical references and index.
ISBN 978-0-7660-3990-2
1. Myers, Walter Dean, 1937—Juvenile literature. 2. Authors, American—20th century—Biography—Juvenile literature. 3. African American authors—Biography—
Juvenile literature. 4. Young adult literature—Authorship—Juvenile literature.
I. Title.
PS3563.Y48Z7 2012
813'.54—dc23
[B]
                                    2011024346
Future editions:
Paperback ISBN 978-1-59845-393-5
ePUB ISBN 978-1-4645-1143-1
PDF ISBN 978-1-4646-1143-8

Printed in China

062012 Leo Paper Group, Heshan City, Guangdong, China

10 9 8 7 6 5 4 3 2 1

To Our Readers: We have done our best to make sure all Internet Addresses in this book were active and appropriate when we went to press. However, the author and the publisher have no control over and assume no liability for the material available on those Internet sites or on other Web sites they may link to. Any comments or suggestions can be sent by e-mail to comments@enslow.com or to the address on the back cover.

Cover Photo: AP Images/Charles Sykes

CONTENTS

Chapter 1

AWARD-WINNING AUTHOR

Walter Myers stood in front of the class and began to read. He tried to read smoothly and clearly, but the words seemed to trip over his tongue. They came out in a rush, a jumble of sounds.

Walter's fifth-grade classmates snickered and made faces. They said things like "He can't talk" and whispered behind their hands. Finally, the reading was over. He had read to the end of the passage; now he could sit down. Angry and embarrassed, Walter made his way back to his seat.[1]

Years later, Myers recalled, "I never understood the source of my speech difficulty. I didn't hear anything unusual when I spoke. I knew what was in my mind but others apparently didn't understand what came out of my mouth."[2]

"They say they have a name for it now, but at the time they just called it mushmouth," he said.[3]

Mrs. Conway, Walter's fifth-grade teacher, understood how difficult it was for Walter to read aloud in class. But despite his speech problems, she could not excuse him from this class requirement. However, she came up with an idea that might make things a little easier. She told the students that if they wished, they could write something of their own to read in class. They did not just have to read from the textbook.

That was a happy day for Walter. "There were many words that I could not, for the life of me, pronounce," said Myers later.[4] He went to work, determined to write something that he could read without difficulty: "I began writing poems so that I could avoid the words that I could not pronounce."[5]

Walter worked hard to find words that fit together in a pleasing pattern but were not hard to say. He left out words that started with *w*, *u*, and *r*. He left out words that had *sh* or *ch* sounds in the middle. These were the words and sounds that gave him trouble, and he was determined to avoid them.[6]

The next time Walter read in front of the class, the words came out smoothly. His tongue did not trip over difficult sounds. His classmates had nothing to laugh at. Instead, they heard a wonderful poem, and they heard praise from the teacher. Walter had written poetry that expressed his thoughts and feelings but used words he did not have trouble saying.[7] He has been writing ever since.

Walter Dean Myers makes his living writing for children and young adults. What started out as a way to keep classmates from laughing at him has turned into a very successful career. His writing has won numerous prizes and awards. He has won the Coretta Scott King Award for African-American writers five times and the Newbery Honor Book award twice.

The first major prize Myers won was for his manuscript *Where Does the Day Go?*, which he submitted to a competition in 1968. He had been writing professionally for many years, but mostly short stories and magazine articles for adults. His work had appeared in several African-American magazines, including the *Negro Digest* and *The Liberator*. He had also written for numerous travel and adventure magazines.[8]

Where Does the Day Go? tells about an African-American father who takes his child and a few others on a walk to the park. As darkness falls, the children wonder where the day goes. Each child tries to answer this perplexing question. After all the children have had a chance to explain, the father tells them what really happens.

Where Does the Day Go? was published as a picture book by Parents Magazine Press in 1969. Prior to this time, Myers had focused his attention on adult writing. Now he began to explore the world of children's literature.

When Myers looked back and recalled the books and stories that he had read in his youth, he could not remember many characters like himself. Most of the children represented in those early stories were white, middle-class children. None of them lived in Harlem, New York. They did not play the kind of games he played or share a lifestyle similar to his.

Where were the African-American children? Where were the brown and black mothers and fathers, calling from doorways or walking to town? Where were people like the ones he saw every day? These people were not present in most of the books he read. According to Myers, "When . . . the overwhelming *absence* of blacks in most books were telling the children of my generation that being black was not to be taken seriously, they were delivering the same message to white children."[9]

The few African-American characters that Myers could remember were caricatures. A caricature is an exaggeration or a distortion of something. The caricatures of African-American people made them look stupid or reinforced negative stereotypes and prejudice.

These images deeply affected Myers. He believed that African-American children deserved better. They deserved books that allowed them to see themselves and their families as they really were. They deserved to see African-American people—mothers, fathers, children—struggling with various problems, sometimes making it and sometimes not. They deserved stories that indicated that the African-American child's world had value.[10]

Myers did not try to pretend that no problems existed, but he also did not let the problems or the environment overwhelm his characters. With inner strength and courage, the characters could succeed. In the stories Myers wrote, he created realistic pictures of his world, his Harlem. He drew on personal experiences to write these stories.

Walter Dean Myers no longer has a speech impediment. His writing is not limited because of specific words or sounds. He no longer lives in Harlem. But his early speech impediment and his life in Harlem have had a profound impact upon who and what he became.

Chapter 2

AN INFORMAL ADOPTION

Walter Milton Myers was born on August 12, 1937, in Martinsburg, West Virginia. His parents, George Ambrose Myers and Mary Green Myers, welcomed him into their large family. They already had two boys, Douglas and George, and four girls, Geraldine, Ethel, Viola, and Gertrude.

George Myers had been married once before, but that marriage ended in divorce. His first wife, Florence Brown, was the daughter of a German immigrant and an American Indian. Her marriage to a black man caused her family to disown her. When Florence Brown and George Myers separated, she left their daughters, Geraldine (called Gerry) and Viola, with their father. She was not sure what she was going to do and decided it was better to leave the girls with him. Later, George Myers married Mary Green.

When their son Walter was about two years old, George and Mary Myers shared some news with their children. There was going to be another baby. The house was small and crowded, and there was little money. What they did have was love and lots of it. They were ready to welcome this new little person into the family.

The Myers family waited for the birth of the baby. Walter waited, too; the baby was going to be his playmate. Unfortunately, something went terribly wrong. Mary Green Myers died giving birth to Imogene. Walter had a new baby sister, but now he had no mother. What were they going to do? George Myers now had eight children to raise and a household to run. How was he going to work and also care for the baby, a toddler, and six other active children?

Life was hard in 1940. The United States was still in the midst of the Great Depression. This was a time when there was little money and high unemployment. The jobs that were available often went to white workers. When blacks were able to find jobs, the jobs tended to be low-paying and required hard, physical labor, and sometimes they were far from home. George Myers pondered what to do. How could he take a job that required him to spend long hours away from home? Who would watch his children?

Family and friends helped out when they could. They brought over food and helped take care of the children. But these people were poor, too; they had their own families. They could do only so much. George Myers was still struggling. Something else had to be done.

In the years that had passed, George Myers's first wife, Florence Brown, had also remarried. She married another African American, Herbert Dean. Florence was much stronger now. Life had taught her some hard lessons, but she was better able to cope with the difficulties that go along with an interracial marriage. Although she did not have much money, Florence was now in a position to care for the two daughters from her first marriage. When she heard about Mary Myers's death, Florence went back to Martinsburg to reclaim her children. George Myers agreed that this was a good time for the girls to go live with their mother.

The Deans arrived to pick up Gerry and Viola. While Herbert Dean was agreeable to bringing the two girls home with them, what he really wanted was a son.[1] Then he saw Walter. Like most children about three years old, Walter ran about the house, getting into everything. He was sweet and impulsive and very much in need of parenting. He had just lost his mother, and his father was overwhelmed. After talking things over with George Myers, the Deans took Walter and the two girls back to New York with them.

Later Walter Myers explained: "Extended families are common among poor people. If a family is experiencing difficulty it is not out of the ordinary for another family . . . to take in one or more of the first family's children. Herbert and Florence Dean took me to raise."[2] Myers described himself as "arriving in New York's Harlem with a snotty nose and wearing a pair of my sister's socks."[3]

The Dean family quickly settled into a routine. The girls went to school, Herbert Dean went to work, and Walter stayed home with Florence. For Walter, this was an idyllic period. On sunny afternoons, he played on the kitchen floor while Florence ironed. Weekdays, when she went to the market and no one else was home, she took Walter with her. It did not take long for him to start calling her Mama. Soon, Florence Dean replaced the mother he had lost.

Florence got a job at a button factory. When she went out to work, Walter stayed with a neighbor. Walter preferred the days when Mama worked at home. On those days, she read to him.

Florence Myers was an avid reader of romance magazines. When she settled down to have a cup of coffee or tea, she would read. Often, she read to Walter. He would sit on her lap or very close beside her while she read aloud. Soon, he was able to pick out words. By the time he was four, Walter could read.[4]

Herbert Dean worked as a handyman and shipping clerk for the U.S. Radium Corporation. To help make ends meet, he picked up extra work as a longshoreman, loading and unloading cargo at a local shipyard. He often worked two or three jobs at a time. He believed in taking care of his family. If it meant working an extra job, that is what he did.

Walter's new father loved to tell stories. He could not read well because he had only completed the third grade, but Herbert Dean could invent the most marvelous stories. He could spin tales that had Walter shaking with fear. Sometimes, Herbert Dean would act as if he were scared, too, and that would frighten Walter all the more.

"I remember one Saturday, Mama had gone [shopping] and my father told me a story about a huge bunny that escaped from a farm and went around looking for bad children. This, of course, meant me," Myers recalled.[5]

"My father could do all kinds of sound effects. He'd kick the table with his foot. That was the bunny coming up the walk. Then he'd slap the table with his hand. That was the bunny on the fire escape," Myers said.[6] "When Dad got to the part about the bunny coming up the fire escape (we lived on the fourth floor) he glanced toward the window, put on his best startled face, and took off running down the hallway of our apartment with me in close and screaming pursuit. We didn't stop until we reached Morningside Park."[7]

Florence Dean also told stories, but her stories were not scary. She told German folktales or stories about real people like blues singer Bessie Smith.

Herbert Dean's father told stories, too. Grandfather Dean told Bible stories. They tended to deal with the wrath of God or consequences of behavior.[8] Storytelling seemed to run in the Dean family.

Often, when children are placed in foster homes, they are not quite comfortable. They feel out of place and wonder whether they will ever find their true home. Not Walter. He felt very much loved by Florence and Herbert Dean. They became his true parents in every way.[9]

The Dean family could be described as poor, but Walter was not aware of that back then. In those days, the definition of poor had to do with being hungry or being cold, and Walter was neither. He was rich in all the things that mattered. He had a loving family and a comfortable home.

Chapter 3

TROUBLEMAKER

Walter trotted off to his first day of school full of excitement. He was already ahead of many of the children who would be in his class. Walter could read, and most of the other children could not. However, things did not go as well as expected.

Walter had a severe speech problem. This speech impediment did not seem to matter at home. His family could always figure out what he was saying, but it soon became clear that others did not always understand him. His speech pattern became a laughing matter. Adult neighbors gave him money just to get him to talk.[1] Then they laughed heartily when his tongue tripped over his words. School was worse. The teachers could not understand him either, and his classmates teased him unmercifully.

The Deans, with help from the school, tried to find the source of Walter's speech difficulties. They sent him to speech therapy.

"Lazy tongue," said one speech therapist. This diagnosis was often pinned on African-American students with speech problems.[2]

"A hearing problem?" another therapist wondered. The assumption was reasonable—Walter would have difficulty speaking if he had difficulty hearing. However, it proved false. Walter did not have a hearing problem; he could hear just fine. Still, the unusual speech pattern persisted.

The only thing that kept Walter from being placed in a special education class was the fact that he was a good reader. He had no trouble following instructions and doing his schoolwork. The teachers said he was a "bright" student.[3] Because he was so smart, they were willing to work with him.

But this bright student soon became a trouble-maker. Although the teachers and counselors were trying to figure out what to do about Walter's speech problem, his classmates were less forgiving. They continually teased him about his speech. They laughed at him, taunted him, and mocked him.

Walter was not about to take this kind of treatment. He had a quick temper and even faster fists. When his classmates started teasing him, the fight was on.[4] Soon, Walter was spending a lot of time sitting in the back of the classroom or in the principal's office. Many times, Mama had to come and get him because he had been suspended from school for fighting.[5]

His parents tried to get him to control his temper. They cautioned him about fighting. They wanted him to ignore the kids and concentrate on school. "You're going to school to get an education," they said.[6] But when the kids started making fun of him, Walter got angry.

Sometimes his parents whipped him when he got into trouble at school. They hoped the whippings would make him stop fighting. "You're not there to rule the teachers," his father would shout.[7]

"They would really whale on me," said Myers, "but I knew exactly what I was getting whaled on for."[8]

Walter also did not like having people feel sorry for him. One day, a teacher was trying to get the class to stop laughing at him. "Now, boys and girls, just give Walter a chance," she had said. This made Walter mad. He thought she was feeling sorry for him, and he threw a book at her.[9] A short time later, Walter was back in the principal's office.

Walter got to be so much of a problem that the school administrators began to think about expelling him permanently. The only thing that saved him from being kicked out of Public School 125 was that he became really sick.

"I was sitting in the back of the classroom waiting for Mama to come when I got sick. When I got home, I was so sick, I threw up."[10] Walter's stomach hurt badly; he could barely stand up. He moaned with pain and clutched his abdomen. His worried parents rushed him to Syddenham Hospital.

"A young doctor said I was okay," said Myers. "But another doctor, she was older, more experienced, said I was not okay."[11] As it turned out, Walter had a bad case of appendicitis. Within the hour, he was prepped for surgery to remove his appendix.

Walter was in the hospital for more than a week. His abdominal incision hurt less as the days passed, though his stitches began to itch. The needle that had been inserted in his vein during surgery was removed. For a few days, all he could eat were clear liquids like Jell-O and broth. When he was able to keep those down without feeling nauseated or vomiting, they advanced him to creamed soups, then to solid food. Gradually, he was allowed out of bed. Eight or nine days passed before Walter was well enough to go home.[12]

Walter spent several weeks at home recuperating. His mother and sisters spoiled him, waiting on him hand and foot. They brought him food and drinks on a tray. They brought books and read to him and played games with him. He enjoyed this period. What he did not enjoy was his trip back to the hospital.

His parents had gone out, and Walter was supposed to be at home—resting. "I sneaked my bike out," said Myers. "I was riding down the street when my father saw me!" Walter raced back home and ran up the stairs. "My incision came open. I had to go back to the hospital."[13]

Walter finished the fourth grade at home, in bed. It was around Easter time when he first became ill, but by the time he was well enough to go back to school, it had closed for summer vacation. When school started up in the fall, his parents enrolled him in another school. The illness was unfortunate, but the timing worked out well for Walter.

Chapter 4

THE MEANEST TEACHER
IN THE SCHOOL?

All was not well for Walter at the new school. The speech impediment was still with him. His classmates still laughed at him and teased him because of the way he talked. But worst of all, he was in Mrs. Conway's fifth-grade class. According to schoolyard gossip, Mrs. Conway was the meanest teacher in the school. Walter soon found out the truth and the fiction about that rumor.

Walter had been fighting again, and the principal decided to suspend him. Someone from the office called Mama, and she was on her way to pick him up. Mrs. Conway told Walter to sit in the back of the classroom and work on his math while he waited. He flipped through his math book. Mrs. Conway moved to the front of the class.

Walter could hear Mrs. Conway giving instructions to the class as he bent forward over his desk. He slipped out a comic book, tucked it in front of his math book, and began to read. Classroom noises drifted back to him as students asked questions, read aloud, or worked at their desks. Now and then, he would look up and peer around the room to see where Mrs. Conway was, then he would go back to reading his comic book.

Suddenly, the comic book was snatched out of his hands. Startled, he looked up to find Mrs. Conway standing over him. She scolded him for not doing his work and reading trash instead. Then she tore the comic book into pieces. Mama arrived a short time later, and Mrs. Conway filled her in on Walter's latest misbehavior. Mama fussed at him all the way home.

When Walter was allowed to return to school, Mrs. Conway brought in a stack of children's books and gave them to him to read. She told Walter that if he was going to spend so much time sitting in the back of the room reading, he should at least read something good. One of the books she gave him to read was a collection of Norwegian folk tales, *East of the Sun, West of the Moon*. These stories were unlike any Walter had ever read before. They opened his eyes to new people, new places, and new adventures. "Reading took on a new dimension for me," Myers said later.[1]

Mrs. Conway also made another change that remarkably transformed Walter's life. She suggested to the class that they might read something that they had written themselves. Walter jumped on this new idea. He knew what sounds and words gave him trouble. He was determined to write something that he could read without his tongue getting in the way. With lots of effort, Walter came up with several poems that he could read without difficulty. His teacher was pleased and his classmates were impressed.

To his surprise, Walter found that he enjoyed writing, especially poetry. "I loved poetry," Myers said later, "poetry . . . around the rhyme. I also did a lot of nature writing then. We were reading that kind of stuff."[2] Walter wrote every day, filling notebooks with poetry and fiction. By the time he was thirteen, Walter would win his first writing contest.[3]

In sixth grade, Walter was one of the biggest students in the school. He had a reputation for being hard to handle, a difficult student. He was assigned to Mr. Lasher's sixth-grade class. Lasher had been in the Marines. He was big and strong and a tough disciplinarian. "I would fight the teachers," explained Myers. "They put me in his class because he could physically handle me."[4]

Lasher used the sixth-grade year to build Walter's confidence. He praised Walter for his good deeds and disciplined him for bad behavior. All the while, Mr. Lasher said what a bright student Walter was. He encouraged Walter to make positive choices. Mr. Lasher's brand of tough love worked, and Walter did well in the sixth grade.

While school had been a struggle, life in the neighborhood was a different story. Walter loved living in Harlem. His boyhood days were filled with fun, and his memories of that time are good ones. His Harlem was a safe place, a place where people raised their families and helped raise the children of others. It was not unusual to be corrected by parents other than your own. "Every adult could grab you on the street and shake you if you were doing something bad," said Myers later.[5]

Myers described Harlem as teeming with life and filled with color. He told of children streaming out of redbrick apartment buildings. He talked about playing with friends in Morningside Park. People knew not only their neighbors, but just about everybody from several blocks around. Harlem was where Myers felt secure; it was a place filled with the best and the brightest of black America.

One of the best was Sugar Ray Robinson, the great African-American welterweight and middleweight boxer. Sugar Ray Robinson was a familiar figure in Harlem. He drew crowds of people most places he went. Myers recalled the time he saw Robinson boxing with some of the boys. "Sugar Ray would come around in a long, lavender Cadillac. He would drive very slowly and yell out the window, 'Get outta my way!' Then he'd get out of his car and box at us!"[6]

Another of Myers's early memories of Harlem was of walking to church on Sunday mornings. The Sunday school teachers stopped by, knocking on doors at various homes, and picked up children for Sunday school. Walter and the other little ones traveled in pairs, holding hands while singing as they walked down the street. When Walter was older, he made the walk to church by himself.

The Church of the Master, just down the street and around the corner from the Myers family's apartment building, was an important part of the Harlem community.

Besides meeting the moral and spiritual needs of the congregation, it also served as a community center. Many cultural and recreational activities took place there.

One of the after-school activities that Walter took part in was a modern dance class. The pastor, the Reverend James H. Robinson, liked to take advantage of cultural resources in the area. He brought in professional dancers from a nearby dance troupe to teach the class. Later, the dance class put on a production inspired by James Weldon Johnson's poem "The Creation." Because he was such a good dancer, Walter got to play the starring role of Adam. One of his brothers, who did not dance well, played the unmoving role of God.

By this time, Walter's biological father, George Myers, had moved his family to Harlem. Walter saw his brothers and sisters frequently, meeting them at the church, school, or other places in the community, but he had little contact with George Myers.

One day Josephine Baker, the famous African-American singer and dancer, put on a show at the church. Walter was impressed. "She had a French accent because she lived in France and spoke French most of the time when she was there. I considered her a foreigner, but what did I know!" he recalled later.[7]

Walter and his friends spent a lot of time playing basketball in the church gym. Outside, they played handball, whacking the ball noisily against the side of the church. Other neighborhood activities included playing baseball at a sandlot on Morningside Drive. Or they played more basketball. Many times, they played basketball in Morningside Park until it got too dark to see. Then they climbed over the fence and went home.

Walter was tall for his age and very athletic. He was good at just about any sport, and because of this, readily accepted in the neighborhood. His speech problems did not matter when he was shooting baskets or slugging baseballs. However, his interests began to shift. He still played ball with his friends, but he also spent more time reading and writing.

One of Walter's favorite places to read was the George Bruce branch of the New York Public Library on 125th Street. He was often there reading and checking out books. These books took him to different time periods and exotic places and informed him about so many things. Walter kept reading and he kept writing, and he began to think about becoming a writer.

Walter's best friend was a German boy named Eric Leonhardt. Their mothers were good friends, therefore the boys naturally spent a lot of time together. The Leonhardts owned a bakery. Whenever Walter visited the bakery, Eric's father gave him chocolate-chip cookies. Another reason Walter and Eric were such good friends was that they were both tall. Because they were so tall, they almost always stood next to each other in lines at school. Walter thought their friendship would last a long time, but as the boys moved into junior high school, things began to change.

Walter and Eric discovered girls. They started going to parties. Gradually, Walter became aware that there were certain parties that Eric was invited to and he was not. Walter realized that the reason he was not welcome at these parties was that he was black.

This social dilemma made both boys feel awkward. Eric was not comfortable knowing that he was invited to places where Walter was excluded. He did not know how to explain to Walter where he had been.

Walter was not happy about it either. He was not willing to be Eric's "colored" friend, acceptable some of the time but not all of the time.[8]

Walter spent more and more time alone. While he was alone, he questioned various areas of his life. Why should people eat meat? He experimented with a vegetarian diet. He wondered about the existence of God. Walter asked himself why he was so different from his parents. Was it okay to stay at home reading instead of hanging out with friends? Was it normal to feel such self-doubt?[9] While he pondered these weighty issues, Walter continued to write and read poetry.

In junior high school, one of Walter's favorite writers was the famous British poet Dylan Thomas. "I liked the rhythm of his poetry," said Myers.[10] He had read Thomas's poetry in class and had heard Thomas reading poetry on the radio. "He had a very distinctive accent," said Myers of Thomas's Welsh lilt.[11] Young Walter decided he wanted to be like Dylan Thomas.

Far from his native Wales, Thomas hung out at a bar called the White Horse Tavern in the Greenwich Village section of New York City. Walter sneaked into the White Horse several times to see Thomas and hear him read. Hidden in a corner or leaning against a wall, Walter watched Thomas covertly. When the bartenders discovered Walter's presence, they threw him out.

Once, Walter even got tipsy trying to imitate his hero. "I was big for my age," said Myers. "I went up to the bar and ordered a beer and I got one."[12] Despite his efforts, Walter never got the opportunity to speak to Thomas. He was too shy to approach the poet.

Walter read many books written by English authors. "There were very few black authors that were popular or accessible in the schools then," said Myers. "We read English authors and we learned to like them."[13]

All that reading and writing had a great effect on his grades. Walter's grades were so good that he went into an accelerated program for junior high students, completing the seventh and eighth grades in just one year. He did so well that his teachers recommended that he go to Stuyvesant High School. Stuyvesant was considered to be one of the best high schools in New York; it had a special focus on math and science. However, math and science were not Walter's strong points. Once again, all did not go as well as expected at the new school.

Chapter 5

SHATTERED DREAMS

The math and science programs at Stuyvesant High School proved to be a struggle for Walter. However, he excelled in reading and writing. For him, the language arts were a joy.

Walter's English teacher, Bonnie Liebow, tried to bring out the best in all her students. To do this, she interviewed each of them and found out his or her interests. Then she made a special reading list for each student.

Mrs. Liebow recognized Walter's potential. She guided him in his reading and encouraged him to write. He entered an essay contest and won. He entered a poetry contest and won that, too, bringing home a set of encyclopedias as first prize. Walter began to think more seriously about becoming a writer when he grew up.

However, the idea of being a writer presented problems for Walter. He was not quite sure that writing was a real job. He also had to consider his father's opinions.

Despite the fact that Herbert Dean was a great storyteller, he did not make his living telling stories. He was a laborer from a long line of people who worked hard to make a living. He did not view writing stories as work; writing stories was something you did in your spare time.[1] While he was proud that Walter had won the essay and poetry contests, Herbert Dean did not see these achievements as being useful when it came to putting food on the table.

But Walter wanted to write. He also wanted a typewriter. "I had seen a writer in a movie with a portable typeteller. I thought it was so cool," said Myers.[2] He decided he had to have one. Walter got a job and started saving his money. He worked after school and on weekends.

Several months later, when Walter thought he had saved enough money, he went to the store to make his purchase. Walter was going to get a portable model like the one he had seen in the movie. He could see himself lifting it out of the sleek carrying case and setting it up on the table. He imagined typing his first piece. He was shocked to discover that he did not have nearly enough money. The model he had chosen cost much more than he had been able to save. Herbert Dean, touched by his son's disappointment, bought Walter a typewriter.

"He went out and bought me this used office model. It was not the kind of typewriter I wanted. I wouldn't touch it for a month." Eventually, Walter got over his sulk about not getting a portable typewriter and began to use the one from his father. "That was a good ol' typewriter," Myers said later.[3]

People in the community made comments to Walter about his reading and writing. While he was trying to save money for the typewriter, one of his jobs had included delivering packages to the post office. Since he read during any spare moment that he could find, Walter usually had a book under his arm when he went to mail his packages. Occasionally, he got wary looks from some of the African-American postal workers. One day, one of them said, "Man, what you got that book in your hands for? You ain't nothin' but another nigger, just like me." [4]

The man's words disturbed Walter. They made him look at his community differently. He realized that many of the African-American men whom he saw everyday, including his father, had low-paying, menial jobs. Walter's thoughts were in turmoil: His teachers were encouraging him to value and pursue education with thoughts of college in the future. However, the people who lived in his community were more practical when it came to making a living. Life's experiences had forced them to be. College was for others, not for them.

Walter wondered just where he fit in. He wanted to go to college and become a writer. But college cost money—lots of money—and his family did not have much of that. There were times when they did not have enough money to buy clothing for school. How would they be able to afford college?

Walter began to reconsider his future. "As I neared the end of my junior year in high school, I saw that going to college would be financially impossible."[5] When he realized that college was not an option, Walter became so disappointed, so disillusioned, that he started skipping school. His dreams had been crushed, his self-image damaged. What good was school?

"I felt my life was falling apart, that I had no control over my destiny," Myers said later. "I also began to recognize that my 'rightful place' might be defined more by my race than my abilities."[6]

When Walter skipped school, he would find a private place and read. Sometimes he read for hours. He used reading to escape, to get away from all the pressures and problems of his life. In his reading, he was not limited to certain places and positions—he could go anywhere, be anybody. In his reading, he was totally free. Walter cut school so much that one day when he showed up, the doors were locked. School had closed for summer vacation.[7]

He started hanging out in the streets and running with a bad crowd. "I got into some really nasty trouble," said Myers. "I ran with what I thought were a cool bunch of guys, but they were really bad eggs. We wanted to be tough guys."[8]

Walter carried a knife in his tough-guy role. One day, he had to use that knife to save his skin. He saw some guys from a gang beating up a kid who had just moved into the neighborhood. Walter stopped the fight. The gang members decided to get back at Walter for his interference. They tried to jump him in the park. Walter pulled his knife and they backed off. He ran for home. Once Walter got there, he was safe. But for how long would he be safe? This encounter with violence scared him.[9]

Another frightening incident proved to be the last straw. Myers and his tough-guy friends hired out their fists: "If someone wanted somebody beaten up, we would do it." However, this time they got more than they bargained for. "My buddy was supposed to beat up a guy and I went along with him," explained Myers. "My buddy was being set up. The guy turned out to be a cop!"[10]

Myers and his friend located their victim in the subway. During the scuffle, the man pulled a gun and identified himself as a police officer. The boys ran. They took off through the subway with the officer in pursuit. The boys zigzagged through crowds of people, pounded up the steps, and escaped.

Walter sneaked home, fearful that he might get arrested. "[The officer] had my buddy's name, but not my name," said Myers.[11] He wondered how long it would take before the police discovered his identity. He was afraid to tell his parents. He knew what they would think about the whole mess. Walter did not know what to do.

While he was trying to sort things out, Walter came across the poem "The Soldier."[12] In it, the English poet Rupert Brooke wrote of fighting for his country and dying in a faraway place. The idea of dying on a distant battlefield seemed somewhat romantic to Walter. The thought that the

Army offered an avenue of escape was even more appealing. "I was sixteen years old and in more trouble than I could handle," said Myers. "I had to get away."[13]

Walter decided to join the Army, but he had to wait a few weeks. He could not join until he was seventeen years old. On his seventeenth birthday, August 12, 1954, Walter joined the service. Seven days later, he was on his way to Fort Dix, New Jersey, for boot camp.

Walter's parents were shocked. They did not know he had enlisted; he did not tell them until the morning he was scheduled to leave. When Walter announced that he had joined the Army and had to leave that very day, his mother sat down and cried.[14]

"My father was more resolved," said Myers. "He knew I'd get into more trouble if I stayed at home."[15] As it turned out, the decision to join the service was a good one. The police came looking for Walter a few days after he left for boot camp.

Chapter 6

THE TOP OF
THE WORLD

Myers completed sixteen weeks of basic training
at Fort Dix. From there, he was sent to Fort
Monmouth, New Jersey, to begin his military
duties.[1] He spent three years in the Army. Myers did not do
any fighting; the United States was not at war. He worked as
a radio repairman, learned to be a soldier, and played lots of
basketball. Life in the Army was fairly uneventful, but he did
get shipped to the Arctic.

Myers's trip to the Arctic came about because his
basketball team lost a tournament. At six feet three inches
tall, Myers was the star on one of the Army intramural
basketball teams. A tournament had been organized, and
Myers's colonel was quite sure Myers's team would win. He
bragged to the other officers about how great the team was,
and he bet a lot of money to back up his talk. Unfortunately,
the team lost in the final game of the tournament. The

colonel was so mad that he had the whole team shipped to the Arctic as punishment.[2] "I was sent up the East Coast, to Baffin Island, past St. John's, through Labrador, to the Arctic Circle," said Myers. "We [the United States] had some missile bases there."[3]

The Arctic includes the Arctic Ocean, which is two miles deep in some spots and covered with ice that is eight to twelve feet thick. It never melts, not even in the summer. The ice just breaks up and floats on top of the water. The ice is never still; the wind and waves keep it in constant motion.

"It's the top of the world," said Myers.[4] The Arctic is the most northern part of the hemisphere. The frozen water of the Arctic Ocean touches the coastlines of eight nations— the United States (in Alaska), the Russian Federation, Canada, Denmark (in its territory of Greenland), Iceland, Norway, Sweden, and Finland.

The Arctic was like nothing Myers had ever seen before. "It was fantastic!" he said later.[5] There was so much ice and snow, and he was amazed by the sounds the ice made. It creaked and groaned as it cracked. It crunched against the sides of the ships. Myers was reminded of the poem by Samuel Taylor Coleridge, "The Rime of the Ancient Mariner." A portion of the poem reads:

The ice was here, the ice was there,
The ice was all around:
It cracked and growled, and roared and howled,
Like noises in a swound![6]

Myers was also fascinated by the animals of the Arctic. He saw the large white polar bears that live on the polar ice cap. He saw seals in their natural habitat. He was interested in the people who made their homes in the harsh environment. Myers had been shipped to the Arctic as a punishment, but it turned out to be a memorable experience instead. He loved the Arctic.[7]

In 1955, Walter Myers received word that his biological father, George Myers, had died. Even though they were not close, Walter quietly mourned George Myers's death.

Myers was discharged from the Army in 1957, when he was twenty years old. He had served his three years and chose not to re-enlist. Myers moved in with his parents, and after some job hunting, he was hired at a local factory. "I got a job twisting cables," recalled Myers many years later.[8]

Florence and Herbert Dean had moved to Morristown, New Jersey, while Myers was in the service. Myers did not like living in Morristown. "It was an old, black community—for the upper classes—and I wasn't upper class," said Myers. "I did not fit in there."[9]

He was also not comfortable living at home again. After having been on his own for the past three years, it was somewhat stifling to be back in his parents' home. They had their own ideas about how people should live. He had to follow their own rules for what went on in their home. Their rules and expectations were not unrealistic, but Myers had gotten used to being on his own, making his own decisions.

"I wanted to try my wings," said Myers.[10] He decided to leave Morristown and the factory job and moved back to Harlem. Myers was surprised by the changes he found in his old community. "Drugs had come to Harlem in a big way," said Myers.[11] It was a different place now, not the cozy, familiar environment he remembered. Harlem was full of pain, disillusionment, and despair. He could not stay there.

Myers found a place to live on 48th Street in midtown New York City. It was a rented room in a run-down hotel. He did not have much money, and he learned to live frugally, spending as little as possible. He rarely bought clothes, and he spent only about two dollars a week on food. Myers lost a lot of weight, dropping almost fifty pounds. Later, he referred to this time in his life as his "starving-artist period."[12]

Myers used this time to read. He spent hours holed up in his hotel room reading one book after another. Eventually, his money ran out and he had to find another job. This time, he worked as the head of a mail room in a brokerage firm.[13]

Myers was not pleased with the work he was able to find. He saw himself as more than a laborer or clerk. "I needed to find a way to identify myself," said Myers. "I needed to find out who I was." He unpacked his old typewriter and started writing again. His work was not selling—not yet—but he was writing. "Even if I was not published, I could identify myself as a writer," Myers said later.[14]

One day, a friend suggested he take the civil service exam. This is a test given to people interested in working for the federal government. After passing the test, a person is eligible to apply for various government jobs. Myers took the test, passed it, and got a job at the post office in 1959.

While working at the post office, the twenty-two-year-old Myers met a young woman named Joyce. He was immediately attracted to her. He asked her out and she accepted. A year later, they were married. Three years later, the Myerses were a family of four. Their first child, a daughter, was born in 1961. They named her Karen Elaine Myers. Their son, Michael Dean, was born in 1963.

Myers kept writing. He wrote in the evening after work, focusing on short stories for adults and on poetry. After Karen's birth, he published some poetry and dedicated the poems to her. During this early period, his work was published in several small literary magazines and several African-American magazines. The *Negro Digest*, *The Liberator*, and *Ebony* are some of the African-American magazines that printed Myers's material.

Despite the fact that Myers was successful at getting his work published, he thought he needed more instruction, and he wanted to surround himself with other writers. In 1961, he signed up for a writing class at a community college. Myers was somewhat intimidated when he compared himself with the other writers in the class. He did not have a college degree. He did not even have a high school diploma. How was he going to hold his own among these people? He thought about dropping out of the class.

The instructor recognized Myers's talent and encouraged him to continue in the class and to keep writing. Myers stuck with it. He wrote several pieces while he was enrolled in the class. Finally, Myers realized that his work was good. His style might be a little different from that of the others, but it suited him.

Myers realized something else, too: He was starting to write what he thought others wanted to read, not what he believed he ought to write. This was something he did not want to do. He did not want to compromise on his work. Feeling much more confident and holding a stronger belief in his work, Myers quit the class.

Working, writing, and family did not leave Myers much spare time. However, one of the things he still enjoyed doing was playing basketball. To stay active, in the early sixties he played on a team called the Jolly Brown Giants. And to relax, he learned to play the flute. When he was learning a new song, Myers would practice it over and over again, often playing the same piece a hundred times before he thought he played it well enough. Myers believed the old saying that practice makes perfect.

Myers worked at the post office for several years, but he was not happy there. Eventually, he was fired, which forced him to look around for something better. Over the next few years, he worked at several different jobs. In 1966, Myers was hired by the New York State Department of Labor as an employment supervisor. However, he was still somewhat dissatisfied with his working life. This dissatisfaction caused trouble at home.[15]

Myers really wanted to be a writer. He wanted to look like a writer and live like a writer—or at least live the way he thought writers lived. He started spending a lot of time in New York City's East Village.

"A lot of artists, writers, and singers were living down there," said Myers. "Alternative newspapers, the Fillmore Theater, and Janis Joplin were down there. The people were struggling but the rents were cheap."[16]

Myers started wearing a beret and played bongo drums at a few East Village clubs. He learned to play the saxophone and the guitar. He stayed out late. "I also drank too much and ran around too much," admitted Myers later.[17]

Joyce Myers was not happy with her husband's new behavior. When she came home from work, she wanted a husband who was home in the evening. She did not want him spending so much time hanging out in the East Village. They began to argue.[18]

Meanwhile, the children, Karen and Michael, were growing, and the family's apartment was too small. After talking it over and looking around various neighborhoods, they decided to buy a house in Queens, New York.

The new house put a strain on finances; Joyce and Walter had difficulty paying all their bills. Soon, both of them were working extra jobs to keep up the payments and meet expenses. The money problems made them irritable. The extra jobs made them tired and even more irritable. Myers continued to run around and stay out late. He and Joyce spent less and less time together and argued more and more.[19]

During this awful time, Myers decided once more to go back to school. He enrolled in New York's City College at night, but he did not do well. Even though he passed French, he flunked English. Myers quit school again, but he continued to write.

Myers wrote short fiction for literary magazines and began to sell some of his work to women's magazines. He found another market for his writing in men's magazines: *Blue Book*, *Male*, *Cavalier*, *Argosy*, and other publications bought articles on kick boxing, bullfighting, travel, and adventure. He even wrote for what some people call the "scandal sheets"—newspapers like the *National Enquirer* and *The Star*. He sold his work wherever he could, sometimes getting paid only $15 to $20 per article.[20]

In 1968, the thirty-one-year-old Myers came across some information about a contest for African-American writers sponsored by the Council on Interracial Books for Children. A manuscript suitable for children was required. Myers wanted to enter the contest, but all the material he had on hand was for adults. So he wrote *Where Does the Day Go?*

Where Does the Day Go? took first prize in the category for three-to-six-year-old readers. It was published as a picture book in 1969 by Parents Magazine Press.

Myers's writing career was moving forward; his magazine pieces continued to sell. "How Long Is Forever?"—a short story—appeared in *Negro Digest* in June 1969. But his newest triumph, the publication of his first picture book, really pleased him. He was thrilled that his first efforts in writing for children had been so successful.

Chapter 7

New Job, Many Changes

Myers continued to work at perfecting his craft. In 1970, at age thirty-three, he enrolled in a writing workshop at Columbia University. The instructor was John Oliver Killens, an African-American novelist and founder of the Harlem Writers' Guild. Killens encouraged African-American writers to expand their horizons and try for new opportunities.

When Killens heard that a local publishing company had an editorial position available, he suggested that Myers apply. Myers was unsure. Some of his old self-doubt came back. No high school diploma. No college degree. How could he get a job as an editor for a book publisher?

John Killens encouraged Myers to apply for the job. He tried to convince Myers that the time was right, that Myers did have the skills to do the job. Killens did not want Myers to miss this opportunity.

"I didn't want to go," said Myers.[1] "My friend accused me of being the kind of black person who is always complaining that he doesn't have a chance. Then, when you give him a chance he doesn't take it."[2]

Killens kept prodding. "Finally, he begged me into going down there and I did," said Myers. "I got the job!"[3]

Myers thought his new editorial job would keep him busy correcting spelling, punctuation, and sentence structure. He was wrong. Bobbs-Merrill Company had other plans for Myers. He was hired to fill the position of acquisitions editor.

As acquisitions editor, Myers was supposed to acquire material for the company to publish. When an author sent a manuscript to Bobbs-Merrill, it was Myers's job to consider whether he thought it would sell and make money for the company. If the answer was yes, Myers discussed the manuscript with others in the office. If the manuscript was approved, after a lengthy process it would be made into a book. The first work acquired by Myers was a book of prose written by African-American poet Nikki Giovanni. When it was published, it was called *Gemini*.

In 1970, Myers's professional life was progressing nicely. He enjoyed his new position. He was learning about the business side of writing in addition to the creative side. Unfortunately, his personal life did not go as well. His ten-year marriage ended in divorce.[4] Joyce Myers retained custody of Karen and Michael Dean. Myers had generous visitation privileges, however, and saw the children often.

He and Michael Dean enjoyed playing ball in the park. One of the things that Myers and Karen did together was shop. "I was responsible for Karen's clothing," said Myers. "And shopping with a girl . . . oh my!" It was a little difficult at first—making sure they bought the right sizes and styles—but Myers found a way to cope. "I'd take her to these nice shops and the women in the stores would help me."[5]

As Karen grew older, she and Myers learned to manage on their own. The shopping trips and the long lunches that sometimes followed allowed them to stay up-to-date on what was going on in each other's lives.

When Myers was not working or spending time with his children, he was busy writing. He published several short fiction pieces in 1971. "Juby" and "The Dark Side of the Moon" were published in *Black Creation*; "The Going On" appeared in *Black World*; and "The Fare to Crown Point" was included in a collection of stories called *What We Must See: Young Black Story-tellers*. He also had a contract with Bobbs-Merrill for a nonfiction book.

Myers decided it was time to get an agent. Since he was working for Bobbs-Merrill and the company was going to publish his book, there was the possibility that a conflict of interest might arise. A conflict of interest can occur if a person's private needs interfere with his responsibility to others. In this case, Myers's private needs regarding rights and payments for the book might have interfered with his responsibilities as an employee of Bobbs-Merrill. The agent handled the contract negotiations for Myers, making sure that both Myers and the Bobbs-Merrill company were treated fairly.

Myers made another major decision in 1971. He changed his name. When he submitted the manuscript for his second picture book, *The Dancers*, he listed his name as Walter Dean Myers. Before, he had always used the name he was given at birth: Walter Milton Myers. Now he adopted the name Walter Dean Myers in honor of the couple who had adopted him.

"I had given my parents such a hard time," said Myers, "but they stuck with me and I turned out okay. I didn't think it was right not to have their name on anything. I decided to include Dean at that point."[6]

Later, Myers was glad he made the name change when he did. *The Dancers* was published by Parents Magazine Press in 1972. By the fall of that year, Myers's foster mother, Florence Dean, was dead. Fortunately, she had a chance to see the book before she died.[7]

The Dancers tells how Michael, a young African-American boy, discovers the ballet. Michael's father works at a theater as a touch-up artist. Michael wants to see where his father works and exactly what his father does, so one day he goes to the theater with his father.

Michael watches as the stage is set for a ballet. He watches the rehearsal and ends up making friends with the ballerina. Michael invites the ballerina to visit his house. There, she dances for Michael and his friends, then eats dinner with Michael's family. After the meal, Michael and his friends teach the ballerina one of their dances, the Funky Chicken. Later, the ballerina arranges for all the children to see her show.

The Dancers got good reviews from the critics. The book was about ballet, but it was not just for girls. It was also a book that boys would read. And, like Myers's first book, *The Dancers* featured a boy and his father. This was important because many books about African-American children showed them with no fathers in the homes.

However, Myers received some criticism about the plot. The critics did not think it was very realistic. They did not believe a ballerina would really dance on a neighborhood street or dance with a bunch of kids.[8]

Did the idea for *The Dancers* come from those dance classes so long ago? "No," said Myers. "I'm just trying to be inclusive. I try to include African Americans in every aspect of life."[9]

Myers's third picture book, *The Dragon Takes a Wife*, was published a few months after *The Dancers*. Unlike *The Dancers*, *The Dragon Takes a Wife* stirred up trouble. Instead of fan mail, Myers got hate mail. He even got a few death threats.[10]

In *The Dragon Takes a Wife*, Myers took a traditional fairy tale and gave it an up-to-date setting. He placed it in the inner city and named one of the key characters Mabel Mae Jones. Mabel Mae Jones is a very untraditional fairy. She is African American and street smart. She says things like "What's bugging you, Baby?" "That knight's a bad dude!" and "I can dig where you're coming from."[11] Mabel Mae Jones created quite a ruckus—in the book and in society.

Some people thought that Myers was helping to stereotype African-American people. They did not like his representing their children that way. Others thought that putting slang in a story made kids think it was okay to talk that way. Myers defended himself by saying that his stories represented the people in his life, in his neighborhood. He said he was telling his own stories and would continue to do so.[12]

Like the dragon, Myers took a wife. In 1973, he married Constance Brendell. Myers and Connie had met years before when both of them worked at the New York State Employment Service.[13] The newlyweds settled in a small apartment. The next year, their son, Christopher, was born.

Myers took two trips abroad with his older son, Michael Dean. In 1974 and 1975, they toured Italy, France, and England. The purpose of the trips was "just to hang out."[14] Myers also went to Greece in 1975 with Connie and baby Christopher.

"That was the year that Chris got tear-gassed," said Myers. "Chris was about six months old. There was a student demonstration going on in front of our hotel and we were standing on our balcony, looking. Connie was holding Christopher. The police came and broke it up. . . . They shot off tear gas and some of the students ran into the hotel."[15]

People were shouting, coughing, and crying. The policemen grappled with students and dragged them out of the hotel. Tear-gas fumes wafted up to the balcony. "Christopher wasn't too frightened at first," said Myers, "and he wasn't hurt. Then he grabbed his mother's face and looked at her. When she started to tear up, he just lost it."[16]

Myers's first nonfiction book, *The World of Work: A Guide to Choosing a Career*, was published by Bobbs-Merrill in 1975. That same year, Myers started writing young adult novels almost by accident. His agent showed one of his short stories to an editor at Viking Press. The editor thought the story was the first chapter of a book, and she liked it.

When the editor saw Myers at a party, she asked him how the story ended. He made up the rest of the story on the spot, and she said she was interested in publishing it. That story became the young adult novel *Fast Sam, Cool Clyde, and Stuff.*[17] A second nonfiction book, *Social Welfare*, was published in 1976.

Myers's writing career was going well. He had moved from children's picture books to young adult novels. His adult feature articles were selling. The future looked bright. Suddenly, all that changed when Myers lost his job at Bobbs-Merrill in 1977. The publishing company was reorganizing and a number of positions were being cut.

Myers, now forty years old, was devastated. Losing his job was hard on his ego and hard on his income.[18] He had three children, Karen, Michael Dean, and Christopher, to support. Where was the money going to come from?

Myers took his time trying to figure out what to do. Since he was already scheduled to take a trip to Hong Kong, he decided to go ahead with it. Connie Myers and Christopher went with him. While there, Myers and his wife talked about the future. They discussed all their options and tallied up their finances.

Myers had received a moderate sum of money from Bobbs-Merrill when he was let go. When that was gone, he could collect unemployment checks for about six months. He had a contract with Viking Press for another book. Myers's ex-wife and Connie Myers both worked, contributing to their families' incomes. By the time Walter Myers, Connie, and Christopher returned home, it had been decided: Myers would not look for another job. He would write full-time.

Now there were new questions: How was Myers going to go about it? What did writing full-time mean? What was a workday? What was included in the work? This was a dilemma for Myers. He had to come up with answers for himself.

First of all, Myers knew that writers do more than just write. They have to come up with ideas for new projects. He wondered whether the time he spent thinking about new story ideas counted as working. As he developed an idea, it often had to be researched. This meant trips to the library looking for information, jotting down notes, and checking out books. Did that count as working? After the research was done, an outline had to be written and files set up to store information. Was that work?

Myers thought about all the things he needed to do, and then he decided that it was all work. But it was only part of the work of a writer. He needed to set specific goals for his workday to feel productive. He came up with this plan: "If I do ten pages [a day], that's work. Ten pages if it's straight fiction. Five to seven pages if it's nonfiction or anything unusual."[19]

The decision had been made: to write full time. The only thing left to do now was write. But write about what? Where would the story ideas come from? Could he generate enough story ideas to make a living and support his family?

As it turned out, Myers did not have a problem coming up with story ideas. For him, it was more a matter of which idea to work on first. In 1977, the year he became a full-time writer, Myers had three young adult novels published— *Mojo and the Russians*, *Brainstorm*, and *Victory for Jamie*.

In 1978, another young adult novel, *It Ain't All for Nothin'*, was published. *It Ain't All for Nothin'* was named an American Library Association Best Book for Young Adults that same year. Myers had another short fiction piece, "The Vision of Filipe," published in *Black Scholar*.

Where do the stories come from? Myers says the stories come from his life, his travels, and his collections. An incident from his childhood might trigger an idea for a book. An item in the newspaper or neighborhood talk may start his idea wheel turning. The people and places he sees and visits bring many other ideas to mind.

Myers's young adult novel *The Young Landlords* is an example of how he takes everyday events and creates a good story. In 1978, Walter and Connie Myers decided their apartment seemed cramped; they needed more room. The family went house hunting.

In New York City, they saw buildings for sale for as little as $25. The buildings were in terrible shape. Windows were broken, roofs were leaking; sometimes the plumbing was missing. Some of the buildings were literally falling down. It would take much more money than they were willing to spend to fix up one of those buildings for their family to live in. Walter and Connie Myers ended up buying a nice Victorian row house in Jersey City, New Jersey.

Later, Myers the writer asked himself a question. What if a bunch of teenagers bought one of the buildings? What would happen then? Myers developed the idea, and *The Young Landlords* was published in 1979.

In addition to *The Young Landlords*, Myers published an essay entitled "The Black Experience in Children's Books: One Step Forward, Two Steps Back." This differed greatly from the material Myers usually wrote.

In the essay, Myers expressed concern about racism in the world of children's literature. He did not believe there was enough good literature that represented all children, and he did not think the publishers cared as much about this issue as they should. Myers stated that the hard-won progress gained during the civil rights movements of the sixties had been lost. He supported that statement by referring to the declining numbers of books being published for black children in the 1970s. The essay got people in the world of children's literature talking.

The Young Landlords was named ALA Best Book for Young Adults. A year later, Myers won his first major award for writing. In 1980, just three years after he started writing full time, Myers won the Coretta Scott King Award for *The Young Landlords*.

The Coretta Scott King Book Award was developed in honor of slain civil rights leader Dr. Martin Luther King, Jr., and his wife, Coretta Scott King. The award is meant to commemorate Dr. King's work to foster peace and brotherhood among all people. It also honors Coretta Scott King's efforts toward the same goals.

The Coretta Scott King award is given annually to an author and to an illustrator whose works best contribute to the world of children's literature. In 1980, the author honored was Walter Dean Myers.

Two more books, *The Black Pearl and the Ghost; or One Mystery after Another* and *The Golden Serpent*, were published in 1980. Altogether, Myers had published four picture books, two nonfiction books, and six young adult novels. His work was well known, and he was picking up major awards. He had been writing full time for only three years. What would the future bring?

Chapter 8

MORE BOOKS, MORE AWARDS

The 1980s brought more changes, more books, and more awards. Some of the changes occurred in Myers's family. His daughter, Karen, had graduated from high school and then attended Queens College in New York. After a while, Karen left school and got married. In 1981, she gave Myers his first grandchild, a baby boy named Brandon. Michael Dean was in his last year of high school and trying to decide his future. Christopher was in elementary school.

Myers had taken trips to South America (1976), Northern Africa (1979), and Egypt (1982). He carefully collected information on the people, the lands, and the legends on each of these trips. In the early 1980s, some of this material became the basis for several books. *The Legend of Tarik*, published in 1981, was set in Morocco. *Tales of a Dead King*, published in 1983, was set in Egypt. Background material for *The Nicholas Factor*, also published in 1983, came from a trip Myers and Christopher had taken to Peru.

The publication of *The Legend of Tarik, Tales of a Dead King,* and *The Nicholas Factor* seemed to indicate a different trend in Myers's writing. This was the beginning of his fantasy and adventure books. These books were not set in Harlem; they had exotic settings in faraway places. Another major change was the racial background of the characters. Prior to this time, Myers's main characters were usually black. However, in *Tales of a Dead King* and *The Nicholas Factor*, the main characters are two white teenagers.

These books were very well received, and two of the three won awards. *The Legend of Tarik* was named an ALA Best Book for Young Adults in 1981 and received the Notable Children's Trade Book in Social Studies Citation in 1982. *Tales of a Dead King* won the New Jersey Institute of Technology Authors Award (1983).

Myers did not abandon the youth of Harlem when he wrote the adventure stories. In 1981, the same year the *Legend of Tarik* came out, *Hoops* was published. *Won't Know Till I Get There* followed in 1982. *Motown and Didi: A Love Story* and *The Outside Shot*, a sequel to *Hoops*, were published in 1984.

Hoops and *The Outside Shot* are basketball stories. They deal with the world of "prime time" basketball players, basketball championships, and relationships. Myers describes the temptations and the problems that go along with being a player of this caliber.

In *Hoops*, Myers introduces Lonnie Jackson. Lonnie and his mother do not get along very well; he feels she is always on his back about something. He will graduate from high school in a few weeks. What will he do then? The chance of college seems remote. The only thing he really feels he has going for him is basketball—he has a great game, but he and the coach do not always agree on how the game should be played.

Lonnie's team is in a championship tournament, and some very shady characters do not want the team to win. These people bet money on the team's losing—and they want Lonnie and his coach to lose the game on purpose. The money offered is tempting but risky. What happens is surprising and frightening.

In *The Outside Shot*, Lonnie tries to make the transition from life in Harlem to a small midwestern college. The people are different; the way basketball is played is different; expectations are different. But there are still shady characters making bets. Lonnie faces disaster when his name comes up during an investigation into illegal betting on basketball games at the college.

Myers knows about betting and basketball from personal experience. He said, "One of the guys I played ball with as a kid got hooked up in a betting scandal."[1] Myers's friend played basketball in college. However, he made some bad choices, took advice from the wrong people, and got involved in a point-shaving scam. "Betting ruined his career," said Myers.[2] Point shaving occurs when a player tries to make his or her team win or lose by a certain number of points.

Motown and Didi: A Love Story was in many aspects about Myers himself. He was Motown and he was Didi. "When I was growing up, I had a love-hate relationship with the black community," said Myers. "That's where *Motown and Didi* came from. Didi wanted to go off to some white college, to get away. Motown wanted to stay and work on the problems.

"I felt the same way growing up. I was bright. I wanted to go to college. I didn't want to be restricted. But, on the other hand, I loved my community."[3] *Motown and Didi* won Myers his second Coretta Scott King Award.

A couple of the scenes in the book bear a strong resemblance to the incident in Myers's adolescence when he rescued a boy from three thugs in a gang fight. When the gang members tried to retaliate later, Myers fought them off with a knife. In *Motown and Didi*, Motown rescues Didi from three attackers. Later, the attackers try to get back at Motown for butting in—and one of them has a gun.

Myers published another picture book, *Mr. Monkey and the Gotcha Bird*, in 1984. He came up with the idea for the book, he said, "as a matter of self-defense."[4] When Christopher Myers was about four years old, the family had taken a trip to Hong Kong. The plane ride was twenty-two hours, and Christopher was not inclined to sit still that long. Myers made up a story to keep his son, Christopher occupied.

In the story, the characters live on an island and talk with a Caribbean accent. Myers entertained Christopher by speaking in the different voices of each character. Myers thumped on the seat, much as Herbert Dean had done when Myers was a boy, to make different sound effects. Years later, Myers wrote the story down, and it was published as *Mr. Monkey and the Gotcha Bird*.

The 1980s also found Myers back in school. He had heard about a college degree program where credit was given for life experience. Students who enrolled in the program contracted to learn certain materials and then spent a year or two doing the work. When the requirements were met, a college degree was awarded. Myers entered the program to gain his father's approval.

"My foster dad was a hardworking man and he always worried about me," Myers recalled. "He'd say, 'Boy, when you gonna get yourself a job?' I thought maybe a degree would impress him and he wouldn't worry so much."[5]

Myers enrolled in the program and took courses that ranged from photography to criminal justice. He spent hours interviewing prisoners confined in a nearby correctional facility for one of his criminal justice classes. After he organized the data from the interviews, Myers wrote a six-hundred-page paper. In 1984, Myers completed the requirements and graduated from New York's Empire State College with a bachelor of arts degree.

"My father was impressed," said Myers. "He said, 'Now, maybe you can get a job!'"[6]

After Myers finished the degree program, he had more time for community service. Christopher had started playing Little League baseball, and Myers now volunteered to help coach the team. He could often be found in Lincoln Park working with the players.

In 1985, Myers became involved in teaching writing at a Jersey City middle school. James Aumack, a teacher at P.S. 40, had read about Myers in the newspaper. Aumack wrote to Myers, inviting him to talk to the students. Myers agreed. One idea led to another, and Myers ended up going to the school twice a month to teach writing to a group of sixth, seventh, and eighth graders.

The students called themselves "The Creative Spirit of P.S. 40." According to Lorraine Kenny, a former Creative Spirit student, "[Myers] taught us about grammar, writing, being creative and how to put it all together."[7] One of Lorraine's stories, "The Vacation," appeared in *Shoe Tree*, a national magazine that publishes children's work. When Lorraine reached high school, she felt comfortable writing the essays and reports her teachers assigned.[8]

Myers encouraged his students to set high goals, and he boosted their self-confidence. By his example, he showed them that a person can come from a disadvantaged background and still do well in life.

Myers then started the Arrow Series, a set of adventure novels featuring two white teenagers, Chris and Ken Arrow. *Adventures in Granada* and *The Hidden Shrine* introduced these two characters in 1985. Myers continued their story in *Duel in the Desert* and *Ambush in the Amazon*, both of which were published in 1986.

Another Myers book, *Sweet Illusions*, was also published in 1986. *Sweet Illusions* was a little different from his usual novel format. This book focused on the problems of teen pregnancy and was unusual because it was an interactive book: Blank pages were provided at the end of each chapter to allow students to write what they thought about the various scenarios presented. *Sweet Illusions* is used in a number of schools to discuss the issue of teen pregnancy.

Myers experienced a personal loss in 1986 when his foster father, Herbert Dean, died. To help cope with his grief, Myers buried himself in work. He wrote two novels, *Crystal* and *Shadow of the Red Moon*, which were published in 1987. He also planned, researched, or made notes on several other projects. And he continued to volunteer his time with the Lincoln Park Little League.

Me, Mop, and the Moondance Kid; *Fallen Angels*; and *Scorpions* were published in 1988. All three of the books made a big impact. All three won awards.

Me, Mop, and the Moondance Kid was inspired by Myers's experiences with Christopher's baseball team. Many of the characters were loosely based on some of the players. "One of the characters was patterned after Christopher," said Myers. "There was a kid in the book that was five feet eleven inches, clutzy—he couldn't handle his being on own feet. Christopher was like that."[9] In *Me, Mop, and the Moondance Kid*, Myers dealt with the theme of foster care and adoption.

Fallen Angels, a novel about the Vietnam War, was a tribute to Myers's younger brother, Sonny. Thomas Wayne Myers, known as Sonny to family and friends, died in Vietnam in 1968. He had been there only two days when he was killed.

Vietnam is a small nation in Southeast Asia. American soldiers were sent there in the 1960s to fight against the spread of communism. The Vietnam War lasted more than ten years. American troops were finally withdrawn after cease-fire agreements were signed in 1973. By that time, thousands of American and Vietnamese lives had been lost.

To some extent, Myers held himself responsible for Sonny's death. He explained:

> I came out of the service wearing a uniform, and my younger brother saw me. He thought it was cool. A few years later, my brother went in [to the service] and he was killed.
>
> People have this really romantic idea of what war is about. Movies make it look cool. You give this dying speech. Get all choked up, then you die.
>
> Brooke's poem "The Soldier" was romantic. Well, war is not like that. It's about dehumanizing your enemy and killing them. Anyone who contributes to that idea [romanticizing war] is wrong. I didn't want to contribute to that.[10]

In *Fallen Angels*, Myers wrote a very realistic description of what happened to a young African-American man who went to Vietnam in 1968. Like Myers, the young man joins the Army at seventeen. The young man, like Myers, is bright. He wants to go to college but he has no money. The Army seems like a good place to go while he figures out his future. A passage from *Fallen Angels* reads:

"My plans, maybe just my dreams really, had been to go to college, and to write like James Baldwin. All the other guys in the neighborhood thought I was going to college. I wasn't, and the army was the place I was going to get away from all the questions."[11]

What the young man found was the horror and reality of war. *Fallen Angels* was named ALA Best Book for Young Adults and received the Parents' Choice Award. Myers also won his third Coretta Scott King Award for *Fallen Angels*.

Scorpions deals with the problems of peer pressure, gangs, and guns. The main character, Jamal, has an older brother, Randy, who is in jail for murder. Randy is the leader of a gang called the Scorpions, and now that he is in jail, the Scorpions want Jamal to take over. Jamal wants nothing to do with the gang, but he is not sure how to avoid them. When someone gives Jamal a gun for protection, Jamal knows it is a bad idea but takes the gun anyway. The gun changes Jamal's life.

Myers said, "When I wrote about Randy . . . I was thinking about a boyhood friend."[12] This sensitive, talented friend, who liked to read poetry, got into trouble and ended up in jail. "When I write about Jamal, I'm trying . . . to show disadvantaged kids how important it is to value themselves."[13] *Scorpions* was named ALA Best Book for Young Adults and earned Myers his first Newbery Honor Book award.

The Newbery Medal is named after John Newbery, an eighteenth-century publisher of children's books. It is given annually to the author who made the most distinguished contribution to American children's literature the previous year. Honor Book medals may also be given; Myers received the Newbery Honor Book award for *Scorpions* in 1989.

As Myers's books became more popular, he was invited to more schools to talk about his work. He spoke candidly, describing, defining, and explaining scenes and circumstances that appeared in his novels. Sometimes, students would come up after the programs and speak privately to Myers. The students had questions or comments they did not want the class to overhear. Many students wrote to Myers. His mailbox began to overflow.

Chapter 9

WRITER FOR THE URBAN TEEN

Myers is one of a very few writers who specifically address the needs of the urban teen. Most of Myers's books are set in Harlem, New York. He identifies the scenes, the conditions, and the problems that teens living in an urban environment often experience. His goal is to make all teens feel that their lives and their environment have value. He offers teens strategies for dealing with difficult situations. Myers gives them hope that they can overcome life's obstacles. The teens respond by writing to Myers.

In their letters, many teens have said that they felt isolated and lonely until they read about a particular character in one of Myers's books. Some tell Myers that they, too, have had a relative in prison. They say they did not know other kids felt the same way they did about having a family member locked up. Reading Myers's books helps them to identify their feelings.[1]

Myers likes getting these letters. He says:

> The letters that I'm most touched by are from kids
> who simply say that the book describes how they
> feel. It removes the sense of isolation. When kids
> find that book, find a good character who makes
> them say look, here I am in a book, this guy feels
> the same way that I do—it's reassuring.[2]

With all this attention from teens, teachers, parents, and award committees, Myers's books have also come under more scrutiny. A characteristic of Myers's work is his use of realistic dialogue. His characters do not always use correct grammar; they sometimes use slang expressions or swear words. Myers has been criticized for this use of language.

There have also been parents and teachers who did not like Myers's choice of topics. They did not want their children or students exposed to the unsavory situations that Myers sometimes addresses. For various reasons, some people have complained to school or library administrators, asking them to remove certain books from the shelves. Removing books because of content is called censorship or banning.

In 1989, *Hoops* appeared on the American Library Association's list of books that had been banned, and *Fallen Angels* appeared on the list in 1990. Profane language or violence is the reason usually given for censorship, but Myers does not always believe that. "I think they don't want black life celebrated," he said.[3]

Overall, Myers thinks that censorship can be a minor thing. "If a book gets a lot of attention, if it's banned, it's more popular. *Fallen Angels* was much more popular after it was banned," said Myers. "What concerns me more is what we are not allowed to publish."[4] Editors have a lot of power in determining which manuscripts are accepted for publication and which manuscripts are not. This can provide a more subtle, more effective means of censorship.

Myers does not let his critics influence his work. In 1990, parents and educators complained about rap music, but the kids embraced it. Myers, knowing this, wrote *The Mouse Rap*. It features a young man called Mouse who enjoys watching television, playing basketball, and rapping. Every chapter in *The Mouse Rap* starts with a rap from Mouse.

Mouse's father works for an oil company in the Middle East and is often away from home. The father of one of Mouse's friends is killed in Lebanon, a small Middle Eastern republic. Around the time *The Mouse Rap* was published, real hostilities were brewing in the Middle East. The presidents of the United States and Iraq had exchanged some harsh words. When negotiations broke down, soldiers were deployed and gunfire erupted. This evolved into the Persian Gulf War.

By this time, Myers's older son, Michael Dean, was an Air Force officer stationed in Turkey, another Middle Eastern republic. Many of the support services provided by the U.S. Air Force in the Persian Gulf War came from Turkey. Turkey was also the scene of war protests and terrorist attacks. Myers's concern for his son's safety was reflected in the references to the Middle East and Lebanon in *The Mouse Rap*.

Myers continued to receive mail from his readers during this time. One letter touched him particularly. It was from a sixteen-year-old boy who had thoughts about fighting in the Persian Gulf War. He followed the news reports closely, taking in the sights and the sounds of the war from his television. "He was so excited he couldn't wait until he turned seventeen to join up," said Myers.[5] After the young man read *Fallen Angels*, he changed his mind.

On February 27, 1991, President George Bush announced a cease-fire; the Persian Gulf War had ended. Several weeks later, American troops were withdrawn, and Michael Dean arrived home safely.

Myers said this about Michael Dean's time in the Gulf: "You hear this story about a woman waking up in the middle of the night in fear, and later she learns that her husband was killed at that exact moment. Well, that's a bunch of crap. The truth is, you wake up every night in fear. It was a very scary time."[6]

In April 1991, Myers was selected "Everyday Hero" by the *Jersey Journal*, a community newspaper. The people named Everyday Hero are chosen because they volunteer to help others. Myers's work with the students at P.S. 40 was just one of the things that got him selected.

Myers added another dimension to his writing in 1991. He published the history book *Now Is Your Time!: The African-American Struggle for Freedom*. Myers had always been interested in black history, but he did not want to just talk about black history, he wanted to document it. "I have to show proof," said Myers. "I want to be able to take any kind of fact and back it up. I want a picture to show or a letter or some kind of document."[7] The desire for proof led Myers all over the world in his search for documents, photographs, and other forms of memorabilia. Some of this material appears in *Now Is Your Time!*

Now Is Your Time! gives a historical account of Myers's biological family while it tells the history of African Americans as a people. Myers said:

> I wanted to do a history book that was not a history of black oppression. It bothers me that many people think black people who succeed are different, an anomaly. I don't like that idea. What I wanted to show is that we do well because we come from loving families and communities that encourage us to do well. I wanted to do the black middle-class experience. Also, my father [Herbert Dean] had died.[8]

Herbert Dean's death caused Myers to think more about his roots, the origins of his family. Many stories had circulated in the Myers family for years. Myers knew the name of the plantation where his family had been enslaved, and he had seen old family photographs. The stories piqued his curiosity enough to lead him to write *Now Is Your Time!*

Now Is Your Time! also tells the story of people like John Fuller, a shoemaker and builder, who purchased his own freedom, then saved enough money to buy freedom for his family too. The book includes a brief history of the landmark

1954 Supreme Court decision in *Brown* v. *Board of Education*, which ruled against segregation in public schools. The book celebrates what African-American people have accomplished.

In 1992, *Now Is Your Time!: The African-American Struggle for Freedom* earned Myers his fourth Coretta Scott King Award.

Christopher had graduated from high school in 1991 and was attending Brown University in Rhode Island. Since Myers became less involved with Christopher, Myers spent even more time writing. In 1992, he published five books—*Somewhere in the Darkness*; *Mop, Moondance, and the Nagasaki Knights*; *The Righteous Revenge of Artemis Bonner*; *Young Martin's Promise*; and *A Place Called Heartbreak: A Story of Vietnam*. He also introduced the 18 Pine Street series.

Young Martin's Promise was another of the history books that Myers was determined to provide for African-American youth. In this book, Myers presents the life of the great African-American hero Dr. Martin Luther King, Jr. Once again, censorship raised its ugly head. *Young Martin's Promise* was banned at a library in Queens, New York.

In 1992, Myers and his wife, Connie, also found time to go to England, where they were able to do research, shop, and relax. Myers described how this annual trip came about. During Christopher's first year at Brown, he came home for the holidays "with a bag full of dirty laundry and a list of parties to go to," said Myers. "Me and his mother said to heck with that!"[9] The couple decided that the next year, they would take a vacation instead of doing laundry, and so they went to England.

Myers was actively involved in promoting his books. He visited schools and talked to students about his books and the writing process. He spoke at libraries and bookstores. Afterward, Myers would answer questions and autograph books. People loved hearing him speak because he was informative, humorous, and articulate.

Unless Myers was telling a joke, people no longer laughed when he talked. The speech impediment that persisted into his midthirties had finally disappeared.

One of the techniques Myers employed to overcome his speech difficulties was to talk in different accents.[10] He particularly liked to use a southern accent. When Myers spoke in an accent or imitated someone else, talking was not a problem. Eventually, with lots of effort, Myers had managed to overcome his speech impediment.

Too much talking soon became a problem. The speaking engagements took up too much time. Writing speeches or developing presentations took time. Traveling to distant cities took time. Myers decided to limit the number of engagements he would accept, and he requested a leave of absence from the writing program at P.S. 40.

In 1993, Myers won several awards and published a poem and two books. *Somewhere in the Darkness* was named a Coretta Scott King Honor Book and Newbery Honor Book. He received the Jeremiah Ludington Award for creating the 18 Pine Street series. His poem "Migration" appeared in a picture book created by African-American painter Jacob Lawrence. Lawrence's book *The Great Migration: An American Story* describes the migration of thousands of African Americans from the rural South to the industrial areas of the North.

Myers continued to write about African-American heroes. In 1993, he published a biography—*Malcolm X: By Any Means Necessary*—and *Brown Angels: An Album of Pictures and Verse*.

Brown Angels was an important work. It was the first of two collections of poetry revolving around photographs of black children and black families. It was followed in 1995 by *Glorious Angels: A Celebration of Children*. The books show the uniqueness of black children and the black family. The books celebrate their lives.

The *Angels* books started with a single photograph. Myers was looking for a picture of a black child to use in a piece he was working on. After a bit of searching, he found what he was looking for and much more. The mischievous looks, sly grins, or serious expressions on the children's faces captivated him.

He kept searching and he kept collecting. Myers found pictures stored in attics and displayed in antique shops. He found pictures in auction houses and carelessly discarded at flea markets. His collection grew. "First there were ten pictures that I cherished, then a hundred, then several hundred carefully tucked away in my files."[11] *Brown Angels* won several awards and was selected as one of the New York Public Library's Books for the Teen Age in 1994.

Chapter 10

LIFETIME ACHIEVEMENT

Myers was rewarded for consistently producing books that represented the urban teen. On February 7, 1994, the Young Adult Library Services Association announced that Walter Dean Myers was the winner of the 1994 Margaret A. Edwards Award. This is a lifetime-achievement award that is given to recognize a body of work, not just one book. The books must help teenagers to better understand themselves and their world.

Myers's work does just that. According to Judy Nelson, chair of the 1994 Edwards Award Committee, "Walter Dean Myers' writing illustrates the universality of the teenage experience in urban America. His authentic portrayal of African-American youth brings joy, empathy and understanding to his readers."[1] Myers was recognized for *Hoops, Motown and Didi, Fallen Angels,* and *Scorpions.*

Malcolm X: By Any Means Necessary was named a Coretta Scott King Honor Book in 1994. Two books, *Darnell Rock Reporting* and *The Glory Field*, were published the same year.

To celebrate the publication of *The Glory Field*, Myers's publisher, Scholastic, Inc., held a small party. Children from the New York City Lab School for Collaborative Studies were invited. At the party, Myers talked a little bit about the book, and the children performed readings from selected portions of *The Glory Field*. Afterward, they ate hors d'oeuvres and Myers autographed books.

A striking portrait of the African-American experience is offered by Myers in *One More River to Cross: An African-American Photograph Album* (1995). The text and the powerful images indicate the people's feelings, like a glimpse into their souls. The impression given is that African-American people have worked hard most of their lives, and they have had times of profound misery.

One photograph shows an elderly black woman standing in a field. She has a long, chopping hoe over her right shoulder. Her left hand clutches a huge basket firmly pressed against her hip. The woman is old, wrinkled, and bent; she looks worn out. The photo depicts the legacy of hard work that is a significant part of the African-American experience. But Myers does not leave his people there. He shows what some of that hard work built—farms, businesses, and towns.

According to Myers, "Blacks were one of the more successful groups. There was a Black Wall Street in Tulsa, Oklahoma. Boley and Langston, Oklahoma. These areas did well up until 1918. Then there was tremendous resistance."[2] Banks denied African Americans loans to expand farms or businesses. Organized hate groups like the Ku Klux Klan and others terrorized African-American communities by beating, burning, and lynching inhabitants.

"I need to show that these things actually happened," said Myers. "With my papers and photographs, I can prove it and I can document it."[3]

Myers also uses this unique photo album approach to show African-American people going about the business of living. His photographs show families in celebration of holidays and special occasions. Young men pose in military uniforms or wade through water fighting America's wars. Children sit in schoolrooms, pose with friends, or eat ice cream on a porch stoop.

He touches on the migration north and the life blacks found there. His pictures show the impact that African Americans have had on style, music, and religion. *One More River to Cross: An African-American Photograph Album* shows the usual and the unusual, the good and the bad. Myers's text describes the African-American experience. The photographs show it.

Myers appeared at a New York City bookstore, Black Books Plus, in 1995. He was there promoting one of his new books and to sign autographs. The store was jammed with people, including a group of students from a college called the New School. Myers settled his large frame on a small chair at the back of the store. The students gathered around him. He talked for a bit and then answered questions.

The questions asked were not unusual. The same questions had been posed by similar groups in similar settings. "How much money do you make?" "What happens to the character at the end?" "Why did you write this book?" "Do you ever get writer's block?" Myers chuckled when one girl asked him how to get published. She told Myers that she had finished writing two books and now all she needed was a publisher.[4] After Myers answered their questions, he signed autographs.

A picture book, *The Story of the Three Kingdoms*, was also published in 1995, and *Shadow of the Red Moon* had been released again. This time, *Shadow of the Red Moon* included illustrations by Myers's son Christopher. It was the first of the projects Myers and Christopher would work on together.

Two more picture books were published in 1996—*How Mr. Monkey Saw the Whole World* and *Toussaint L'Ouverture*. *Toussaint L'Ouverture* was another biography of a black hero, but this one was for younger readers. Two other books made their debut in 1996: *Smiffy Blue: Ace Crime Detective*, aimed at younger readers, and *Slam!*, Myers's newest young adult novel. *Slam!* turned out to be another award winner. In 1997, Myers won his fifth Coretta Scott King Award for this book.

Myers and Christopher worked together again on a 1997 picture book, *Harlem*. Myers created the text, a beautiful poem describing the colors, the rhythms, and the people of Harlem. He wrote about the Harlem he knew well, a Harlem filled with life, love, laughter, and sometimes despair.

Christopher Myers painted the pictures, which are his interpretation of his father's words. Christopher's vision of Harlem worked well. The colors he chose—rich browns and reds, bold blues and yellows—created memorable images. *Harlem* was selected as a Coretta Scott King Honor Book and a Caldecott Honor Book in the illustrator category for 1998.

Myers is proud of this young illustrator who is also his son. "It was fun working with him," said Myers.[5] Christopher, too, enjoys their artistic relationship. "I'm excited working with my pop and I respect him as an artist," he said. "It's been interesting as I grow older to watch our relationship as artists grow. We're making two narratives which parallel—his words with my pictures."[6]

In 1997, the Myers duo visited the Family Academy of New York, a private school located in the city's West Harlem area. Myers talked to the students about writing, and Christopher talked about illustrating. Myers told how stories are developed, Christopher drew sketches at an easel. The schoolchildren were impressed, especially when they saw some of Christopher's early drawings.

"His mother had saved drawings from when Christopher was little," said Myers. "The kids saw Chris's drawings from when he was about four, five, or six years old. They saw pictures from a kid who drew like they draw. Now they see Christopher as a man and an illustrator."[7] They can see what is possible. Myers believes that once the possibilities are revealed, children can choose their destiny.

Extensive reading and research led Myers to information about a mutiny aboard a slave ship. In 1839, a group of Africans had been captured and later imprisoned aboard the slave ship *Amistad*. The African captives broke their bonds and took over the ship. They killed the captain and most of the ship's crew. The Africans were not able to sail back to Africa and were forced to land in the United States. When the *Amistad* docked in New London, Connecticut, the Africans were arrested for piracy and murder. After three years of imprisonment and a lengthy trial, the Africans were found not guilty, and they were given their freedom.

In 1998, Myers wrote *Amistad: A Long Road to Freedom* to document the Africans' struggle. This factual account detailed the capture of the Africans, their journey aboard the slave ship, the mutiny, the arrest, and the three-year court battle.

In addition to *Amistad*, a third book in the Angel series, *Angel to Angel: A Mother's Gift of Love*, was published in 1998. Myers also took time out of his busy schedule to speak at a writer's conference in Chicago, Illinois. In May, he and his wife took one of their many trips. This time, they traveled to Germany and the Netherlands.

Myers had been invited to Germany to visit a number of schools. Because of the American military and diplomatic presence, Germany has quite a few American schools. Myers spent five days discussing his books and talking to schoolchildren about writing. After that, his time was his own.

Next, the couple went to Amsterdam in the Netherlands. There they did all the things that tourists do—sightseeing, shopping, and eating at fine restaurants. Myers also did some work. He collected background material for another book.

Not surprisingly, Myers had a number of books ready for publication in 1999: *Monster: A Novel* and three nonfiction works, *At Her Majesty's Request: An African Princess in Victorian England*; *My Name Is America: Journal of Joshua Loper, A Black Cowboy*; and *My Name Is America: Journal of Scott Pendleton Collins, A WWII Soldier*. *Monster* went on to be nominated for a National Book Award and win a Coretta Scott King Award Honor.

In the twenty-first century, Myers continued to be very prolific. His books included a biography of boxer Muhammad Ali; the novels *Shooter*, *The Beast*, and *Dopesick*; and a modern interpretation of the ballet *Swan Lake* called *Amiri & Odette*. He was even nominated for two more National Book Awards, for *Autobiography of My Dead Brother* (2005), about a Harlem teen who draws in order to deal with his problems, and *Lockdown* (2010), about a youth in a juvenile corrections facility. *Lockdown* also was selected for a Coretta Scott King Award Honor.

Chapter 11

THE POWER OF STORIES

Walter Dean Myers has a secret for success. "The secret," he says, "is discipline and work." He believes that those who do the work are rewarded. "People who are successful writers write an enormous amount of material," said Myers.[1] And that is what he does. He writes just about every day, producing two or more books a year. If the weather is agreeable, Myers starts his day with a walk, sometimes walking five miles. Then he heads for his office to work.

Myers works in a tiny room that was the nursery when Christopher was little. Myers did not bother to redecorate, and his office is not fancy. When the nursery furniture was moved out, the office furniture was moved in. The airplane wallpaper from Christopher's preschool days did not distract Myers a bit. He hung a photo of African-American jazz singer Billie Holiday on the wall, and the office was ready.

His family proved to be very helpful in the development of story ideas. "When Christopher was younger, I'd ask him to read stuff or I'd hire neighborhood kids to read," said Myers.[2] He discovered how the youngsters reacted to certain characters and situations. Spending time with his children and their friends helped him understand what kind of problems they had. Listening to them talk helped Myers write realistic dialogue.

When working up a new idea, Myers often asked his wife, "What do you think of this?" Connie Myers did not hesitate to give her opinion. Sometimes, her comments generated a lively discussion. When the manuscript was complete, she checked it over for details.

Over the years, Connie Myers has become more involved in many areas of Myers's writing life. She knows where all his books are. When he asks, "Connie, where did I put that book on . . . ," she tells him where to find it. She keeps track of his photographs by filing them in a special cabinet for easy retrieval.

"Walter's work has taken over our house," said Connie Myers.[3] Books and photographs are everywhere—in the living room and in the dining room. Visitors have to ease past boxes of books in the hall. Historical, heirloom-type photographs are stacked against a wall or lean against the piano. Even the kitchen is a part of Myers's work environment. That is where he keeps the fax machine and his calendars.

Myers refers to the calendars as "my kitchen schedule and my master schedule."[4] The kitchen schedule is not a list of chores but a list of writing projects. It keeps him up-to-date and on task. He sets specific goals for each day and each week.

A goal on the kitchen schedule might read, "Complete chapter two on *Monster*" or "Write poem for *Angel to Angel*." When a task is completed, Myers marks it off. The kitchen schedule allows him to measure progress toward the goals and deadlines set on his master schedule.

The master schedule is much more comprehensive. It details each project, giving deadlines and setting goals. Future projects are also listed. A date may be marked to start working on a particular piece. An example of a goal for this area might be, "Complete *Slam!* manuscript by . . ." or "Begin research on black cowboys on . . ."[5]

Myers needs these schedules because he has so many projects to keep track of. "I work on more than one project at a time," said Myers. "Some are in the planning stage, some are in the writing stage, and some are in the rewriting stage."[6]

When Myers starts a new project, he carefully plans and outlines the piece. "If I take the time to plan the book really well, the writing goes quickly," said Myers.[7] After he plans the work and develops the outline, he writes the first draft, which is a rough sketch of the story. When the first draft is completed, Myers has a good idea of how the piece is going to go. Then he starts his rewrite phase. Rewriting takes much longer. In this phase, Myers takes care of any problems he identified in the first draft.

Myers develops characters that children can easily relate to. "I spend a lot of time working on characters," said Myers. "I start off with a résumé."[8] A résumé tells the character's story—how old he is, who his family is, where he lives, and the kind of life he has had. This is especially important if the character is a bad guy. Myers does not believe in putting a bad guy in a piece without explaining how he got to be that way. "If a person is a crack addict . . . what you have to do is say why this person is a crack addict," said Myers.[9]

Once the history is established, Myers tries to fix the characters in his mind. He does this by searching through magazines, books, and his photo collection, looking for pictures that represent each character. When he has found them, Connie Myers takes the photos and makes a collage.

Myers hangs the collage in his office. When he is writing, the collage helps him to stay focused. "I can just look up there and my characters are right there," said Myers. "It gets me in the mood [to write]."[10]

Myers puts a lot of thought into the names he chooses for these characters. Sometimes he uses his children's names. Sometimes he uses the names of old friends or past schoolteachers. This helps him to immediately picture a particular character.

Other sources for names are basketball or baseball team rosters and school yearbooks. When Myers visits a school, he often picks up a copy of the yearbook. Later, he looks through the yearbook to find names. However, Myers applies this technique cautiously. "If the character's a bad guy, a drug addict,

I think carefully about the names I choose."[11] These names may describe the character in some way. In *Motown and Didi*, Touchy was a bad guy who did not like to be touched. In *Slam!* Ice was a cold-hearted drug dealer.

Myers brings reality to his novels by incorporating portions of his life into his stories. He might introduce a scene where a girl is having her hair done in the kitchen on Sunday morning. He might describe the sound of a hot curling iron clicking or the smell of singed hair. In *Slam!* he describes the mother washing collard greens in the sink. In *Scorpions*, he describes a girl putting Vaseline on her face.

These were things Myers remembered from his youth, a shared experience with many African-American children. According to Myers, "You put that kind of thing in, not from any conscious deliberation, but because it's what you remember. It's your cultural fabric."[12] Young people pick up on these small, seemingly insignificant details, and they recognize their own experiences.

Myers recalled talking with a group of kids at a Brooklyn school. "One of them said, 'I don't read black books. They always show us beaten up or beaten down. I don't wanna read that stuff all the time.'"[13] Myers thought about what that child said. He realized that many books do feature blacks as victims. He chose to write from a different perspective. His books show that there is more than one way to deal with a problem; it is up to the character to choose. "I write to give hope to those kids who are like the ones I knew—poor, troubled, treated indifferently by society, sometimes bolstered by family and many times not," said Myers.[14]

Myers believes that people learn from stories. He makes this point clearly in his 1995 picture book *The Story of the Three Kingdoms*. The book tells how people triumphed over the rulers of the forest, the sea, and the air. They triumphed because they worked together and learned from the past. A passage from *The Story of the Three Kingdoms reads*:

> We have done this by sitting by the fire and telling stories of what has happened to us, and learning from them. Only we, among all creatures, have the gift of story and the wisdom it brings.[15]

Walter Dean Myers is part of a family of storytellers. Christopher Myers describes his family's tradition this way:

> My grandfather's hands were strong hands. The rough, thick hands of a man who worked hard all his life. Those hands told stories. Funny stories. Those hands could make you scared.
>
> I think about my great-grandfather's hands. Strong hands. Farmer's hands. Hands that moved earth. Those hands told stories, too. Biblical stories.
>
> Then I think about my father's hands. My father's hands are very soft. His hands move words. His hands tell stories. And then, there are my hands. My hands make stories with pictures. It's all about the power of stories. Telling stories and learning from our history.[16]

The stories and the learning will go on. According to Walter Dean Myers, "There is always one more story to tell, one more person whose life needs to be held up to the sun."[17]

CHRONOLOGY

1937—Walter Milton Myers is born on August 12 in Martinsburg, West Virginia.

1940—Walter's mother dies; he is informally adopted by Florence and Herbert Dean and moves to Harlem, New York.

1954—Joins the United States Army.

1955—Death of biological father, George Myers.

1957—Receives discharge from the Army.

1959—Works at the post office.

1960—Marries for first time.

1961—Daughter, Karen, is born; Myers publishes poetry in a literary magazine.

1963—Son Michael Dean is born; Myers begins writing for African-American and men's magazines.

1968—*Where Does The Day Go*? wins first prize in a writing contest sponsored by the Council on Interracial Books for Children.

1969—*Where Does The Day Go*? is published as a picture book by Parents Magazine Press.

1970—Becomes an editor at Bobbs-Merrill publishing company; first marriage breaks up.

1971—Changes name to Walter Dean Myers.

1972—Foster mother, Florence Dean, dies.

1973—Marries Constance Brendell.

1974—Son Christopher is born.

1975—First young adult novel, *Fast Sam, Cool Clyde, and Stuff*, is published; first nonfiction book, *The World of Work*, is published.

1977—Leaves Bobbs-Merrill and decides to write full time.

1978—*It Ain't All For Nothin'* is named American Library Association (ALA) Best Book for Young Adults.

1979—*The Young Landlords* is selected ALA Best Book for Young Adults.

1980—Receives Coretta Scott King Award for *The Young Landlords*.

1981—*The Legend of Tarik* is named ALA Best Book for Young Adults.

1982—*Hoops* is named ALA Best Book for Young Adults.

1984—Earns bachelor of arts degree from New York's Empire State College.

1985—Receives the Coretta Scott King Award for *Motown and Didi: A Love Story*.

1986—Foster father, Herbert Dean, dies.

1988—Receives ALA Notable Book citations for *Scorpions* and for *Me, Mop, and the Moondance Kid*. *Fallen Angels* and *Scorpions* are named ALA Best Book for Young Adults.

1989—Receives Coretta Scott King Award for *Fallen Angels*; *Scorpions* is chosen as a Newbery Honor Book.

1992—Receives the Coretta Scott King Award for *Now Is Your Time!*

1993—*Somewhere in the Darkness* is named Coretta Scott King Honor Book and Newbery Honor Book; *Brown Angels* is selected by *Parenting* magazine as one of the Ten Best Books for 1993.

1994—Receives Margaret A. Edwards Award for lifetime achievement; *Malcolm X: By Any Means Necessary* is named Coretta Scott King Honor Book. *Brown Angels* is named ALA Notable Children's Book and one of the New York Public Library's Books for the Teen Age.

1997—Receives Coretta Scott King Award for *Slam!*; *Harlem* is named Boston Globe--Horn Book Honor Book.

1999—*Monster* is nominated for a National Book Award and wins a Coretta Scott King Award Honor.

2005—Nominated for a National Book Award for *Autobiography of My Dead Brother*.

2007—Son Christopher wins a Coretta Scott King Illustrator Award for *Jazz*, for which Walter Dean Myers wrote the text.

2010—Nominated for a National Book Award for *Lockdown*; wins a Coretta Scott King Award Honor for that book as well.

BOOKS BY
WALTER DEAN MYERS

A Selected List
Picture Books

Where Does the Day Go? 1969
The Dragon Takes A Wife, 1972
The Dancers, 1972
Fly, Jimmy, Fly, 1974
Mr. Monkey and the Gotcha Bird, 1984
The Story of the Three Kingdoms, 1995
How Mr. Monkey Saw the Whole World, 1996
Toussaint L'Ouverture: The Fight for Haiti's Freedom, 1996
Harlem, 1997

Biographies

Young Martin's Promise, 1993
Malcolm X: By Any Means Necessary, 1993
At Her Majesty's Request: An African Princess in Victorian England, 1999
My Name Is America: Journal of Joshua Loper, A Black Cowboy, 1999
My Name Is America: Journal of Scott Pendleton Collins, A WWII Soldier, 1999
Greatest: Muhammad Ali, 2001
Bad Boy: A Memoir, 2002

Photo-History/Photo-Poetry Books

Now Is Your Time!: The African-American Struggle for Freedom, 1991

Brown Angels: An Album of Pictures and Verse, 1993

Glorious Angels: A Celebration of Children, 1995

One More River to Cross: An African-American Photograph Album, 1995

Angel to Angel: A Mother's Gift of Love, 1998

Novels

Fast Sam, Cool Clyde, and Stuff, 1975

Brainstorm, 1977

Mojo and the Russians, 1977

Victory for Jamie, 1977

It Ain't All for Nothin', 1978

The Young Landlords, 1979

The Black Pearl and the Ghost; or One Mystery After Another, 1980

The Golden Serpent, 1980

Hoops, 1981

The Legend of Tarik, 1981

Won't Know Till I Get There, 1982

The Nicholas Factor, 1983

Tales of a Dead King, 1983

Motown and Didi: A Love Story, 1984

The Outside Shot, 1984

Sweet Illusions, 1986

Crystal, 1987

Shadow of the Red Moon, 1997

Fallen Angels, 1988

Scorpions, 1988

Me, Mop, and the Moondance Kid, 1988

The Mouse Rap, 1990

Somewhere in the Darkness, 1992

The Righteous Revenge of Artemis Bonner, 1992

Mop, Moondance, and the Nagasaki Nights, 1992

Darnell Rock Reporting, 1994

The Glory Field, 1994

Slam!, 1996

Smiffy Blue: Ace Crime Detective, 1996

Monster: A Novel, 1999

Handbook for Boys, 2003

The Beast, 2003

Shooter, 2004

Autobiography of My Dead Brother, 2005

Game, 2008

Dopesick, 2009

Amiri & Odette, 2009

Lockdown, 2010

Nonfiction

A Place Called Heartbreak: A Story of Vietnam, 1992

Amistad: A Long Road to Freedom, 1998

CHAPTER NOTES

Chapter 1. Award-Winning Author

1. Personal interview with Walter Dean Myers, August 1, 1997.

2. *Authors and Artists for Young Adults*, vol. 4 (Detroit: Gale Research, Inc., 1990), p. 206.

3. Amanda Smith, "Walter Dean Myers: This Award-Winning Author for Young People Tells It Like It Is," *Publishers Weekly*, July 20, 1992, p. 217.

4. *Authors and Artists for Young Adults*, p. 206.

5. Ibid.

6. Rudine Sims Bishop, *Twayne's United States Author Series: Presenting Walter Dean Myers* (Boston: Twayne Publishers, 1991), p. 5.

7. "Meet: Walter Dean Myers, Making Intellect Cool," *NEA Today*, December 1991, p. 9.

8. Roger Sutton, "Threads in Our Cultural Fabric: A Conversation With Walter Dean Myers," *School Library Journal*, June 1994, p. 27.

9. *Authors and Artists for Young Adults*, p. 210.

10. Walter Dean Myers, "The Black Experience in Children's Books: One Step Forward, Two Steps Back," *Interracial Books for Children Bulletin*, vol. 10, no. 6, 1979, p. 15.

Chapter 2. An Informal Adoption

1. Rudine Sims Bishop, *Twayne's United States Author Series: Presenting Walter Dean Myers* (Boston: Twayne Publishers, 1990), p. 2.

2. *Authors and Artists for Young Adults*, vol. 4 (Detroit: Gale Research, Inc., 1990), p. 205.

3. Ibid.

4. Bishop, p. 3.

5. *Authors and Artists for Young Adults*, p. 205.

6. Personal interview with Walter Dean Myers, March 18, 1998.

7. *Authors and Artists for Young Adults*, p. 205.

8. Personal interview with Christopher Myers, March 18, 1998.

9. Personal interview with Walter Dean Myers, August 1, 1997.

Chapter 3. Troublemaker

1. Rudine Sims Bishop, *Twayne's United States Author Series: Presenting Walter Dean Myers* (Boston: Twayne Publishers, 1991), p. 4.

2. Ibid.

3. Ibid.

4. Personal interview with Walter Dean Myers, August 1, 1997.

5. Ibid.

6. Personal interview with Walter Dean Myers, February 4, 1998.

7. Ibid.

8. Ibid.

9. Bishop, p. 5.

10. Personal interview with Walter Dean Myers, February 4, 1998.

11. Ibid.

12. Ibid.

13. Ibid.

Chapter 4. The Meanest Teacher in the School?

1. *Something About the Author Autobiography Series*, vol. 41 (Detroit: Gale Research, Inc., 1985), p. 153.

2. Personal interview with Walter Dean Myers, February 4, 1998.

3. Ibid.

4. Personal interview with Walter Dean Myers, March 18, 1998.

5. Amanda Smith, "Walter Dean Myers: This Award-Winning Author for Young People Tells It Like It Is," *Publishers Weekly*, July 20, 1992, p. 217.

6. Personal interview with Walter Dean Myers, February 4, 1998.

7. Ibid.

8. *Authors and Artists for Young Adults*, vol. 4 (Detroit: Gale Research, Inc., 1990), p. 208.

9. Walter Dean Myers, "1994 Margaret A. Edwards Award Acceptance Speech," *Youth Services in Libraries*, winter 1995, p. 131.

10. Personal interview with Walter Dean Myers, February 4, 1998.

11. Personal interview with Walter Dean Myers, August 1, 1997.

12. Personal interview with Walter Dean Myers, March 18, 1998.

13. Personal interview with Walter Dean Myers, February 4, 1998.

Chapter 5. Shattered Dreams

1. Rudine Sims Bishop, *Twayne's United States Author Series: Presenting Walter Dean Myers* (Boston: Twayne Publishers, 1991), p. 8.

2. Personal interview with Walter Dean Myers, March 18, 1998.

3. Ibid.

4. *Authors and Artists for Young Adults*, vol. 4 (Detroit: Gale Research, Inc., 1990), p. 208.

5. *Biography Today 1993 Annual Cumulation* (Detroit: Omnigraphics, Inc., 1994), p. 224.

6. Ibid.

7. Bishop, pp. 7–8.

8. Personal interview with Walter Dean Myers, February 4, 1998.

9. Ibid.

10. Ibid.

11. Personal interview with Walter Dean Myers, March 18, 1998.

12. Bishop, p. 9.

13. Personal interview with Walter Dean Myers, February 4, 1998.

14. Ibid.

15. Ibid.

Chapter 6. The Top of the World

1. Personal interview with Walter Dean Myers, February 4, 1998.

2. Elizabeth Mehren, "Fountain of Stories for Youth: Walter Dean Myers," *The Los Angeles Times*, October 15, 1997, p. E1.

3. Personal interview with Walter Dean Myers, March 18, 1998.

4. Ibid.

5. Ibid.

6. Samuel T. Coleridge, *The Poetical Works of Coleridge* (London: Oxford University Press, 1969), p. 189.

7. Mehren, p. E1.

8. Personal interview with Walter Dean Myers, August 1, 1997.

9. Personal interview with Walter Dean Myers, February 4, 1998.

10. Ibid.

11. *Authors and Artists for Young Adults*, vol. 4 (Detroit: Gale Research, Inc., 1990), p. 209.

12. Rudine Sims Bishop, *Twayne's United States Author Series: Presenting Walter Dean Myers* (Boston: Twayne Publishers, 1991), p. 9.

13. Personal interview with Walter Dean Myers, August 1, 1997.

14. Ibid.

15. *Authors and Artists for Young Adults*, p. 209.

16. Personal interview with Walter Dean Myers, March 18, 1998.

17. Ibid.

18. *Authors and Artists for Young Adults*, p. 209.

19. Ibid., p. 210.

20. Mehren, p. E1.

Chapter 7. New Job, Many Changes

1. Personal interview with Walter Dean Myers, February 4, 1998.

2. Elizabeth Mehren, "Fountain of Stories for Youth: Walter Dean Myers," *The Los Angeles Times*, October 15, 1997, p. E1.

3. Personal interview with Walter Dean Myers, February 4, 1998.

4. Personal interview with Walter Dean Myers, September 4, 1998.

5. Ibid.

6. Personal interview with Walter Dean Myers, March 18, 1998.

7. Personal interview with Walter Dean Myers, September 4, 1998.

8. Rudine Sims Bishop, *Twayne's United States Author Series: Presenting Walter Dean Myers* (Boston: Twayne Publishers, 1991), p. 12.

9. Personal interview with Walter Dean Myers, March 18, 1998.

10. Mehren, p. E1.

11. Walter Dean Myers, *The Dragon Takes a Wife* (New York: Bobbs-Merrill, 1972).

12. Roger Sutton, "Threads in Our Cultural Fabric: A Conversation With Walter Dean Myers," *School Library Journal*, June 1994, p. 25.

13. Personal interview with Walter Dean Myers, August 1, 1997.

14. Personal interview with Walter Dean Myers, September 4, 1998.

15. Personal interview with Walter Dean Myers, November 6, 1998.

16. Ibid.

17. Amanda Smith, "Walter Dean Myers: This Award-Winning Author for Young People Tells It Like It Is," *Publishers Weekly,* July 20, 1992, p. 217.

18. *Authors and Artists for Young Adults*, vol. 4 (Detroit: Gale Research, Inc., 1990), p. 212.

19. Personal interview with Walter Dean Myers, August 1, 1997.

Chapter 8. More Books, More Awards

1. Personal interview with Walter Dean Myers, March 18, 1998.

2. Ibid.

3. Ibid.

4. Ibid.

5. Personal interview with Walter Dean Myers, September 4, 1998.

6. Ibid.

7. Keith Sharon, "Ordinary Guy Calls Forth Creative Spirits," *The Jersey Journal*, April 11, 1991, p. 17.

8. Ibid.

9. Personal interview with Walter Dean Myers, September 4, 1998.

10. Personal interview with Walter Dean Myers, March 18, 1998.

11. Walter Dean Myers, *Fallen Angels* (New York: Scholastic, Inc., 1988), p. 15.

12. Shirley Horner, "Author Seeks to Inspire Black Youth," *The New York Times*, August 21, 1988, sec. 12, p. 10.

13. Ibid.

Chapter 9. Writer for the Urban Teen

1. Personal interview with Walter Dean Myers, August 1, 1997.

2. Roger Sutton, "Threads in Our Cultural Fabric: A Conversation With Walter Dean Myers," *School Library Journal*, June 1994, p. 28.

3. Personal interview with Walter Dean Myers, March 18, 1998.

4. Personal interview with Walter Dean Myers, September 4, 1998.

5. Amanda Smith, "Walter Dean Myers: This Award-Winning Author for Young People Tells It Like It Is," *Publishers Weekly*, July 20, 1992, p. 218.

6. Personal interview with Walter Dean Myers, September 4, 1998.

7. Personal interview with Walter Dean Myers, August 1, 1997.

8. Personal interview with Walter Dean Myers, March 18, 1998.

9. Personal interview with Walter Dean Myers, November 6, 1998.

10. Personal interview with Walter Dean Myers, February 4, 1998.

11. Walter Dean Myers, introduction to *Brown Angels: An Album of Pictures and Verse* (New York: HarperCollins, 1993).

Chapter 10. Lifetime Achievement

1. "Walter Dean Myers Named Margaret A. Edwards Award Recipient," *American Library Association* press release, February, 1994, p. 1.

2. Personal interview with Walter Dean Myers, August 1, 1997.

3. Ibid.

4. Laurence Chollet, "A Teller of Tales Re-creating the Past for the Children of Today," *The New Jersey Record*, January 22, 1995, p. E01.

5. Personal interview with Walter Dean Myers, March 18, 1998.

6. Personal interview with Christopher Myers, March 18, 1998.

7. Personal interview with Walter Dean Myers, March 18, 1998.

Chapter 11. The Power of Stories

1. Personal interview with Walter Dean Myers, August 1, 1997.

2. Ibid.

3. Personal interview with Constance Myers, August 1, 1997.

4. Personal interview with Walter Dean Myers, August 1, 1997.

5. Ibid.

6. Ibid.

7. Ibid.

8. Jim Naughton, "Walter Dean Myers, Writing About Reality for Black Children," *The Washington Post*, December 9, 1989, p. C01.

9. Roger Sutton, "Threads in Our Cultural Fabric: A Conversation With Walter Dean Myers," *School Library Journal*, June 1994, p. 25.

10. Personal interview with Walter Dean Myers, March 18, 1998.

11. Ibid.

12. Sutton, p.26.

13. Personal interview with Walter Dean Myers, August 1, 1997.

14. Shirley Horner, "Author Seeks to Inspire Black Youth," *The New York Times*, August 21, 1988, sec. 12, p. 10.

15. Walter Dean Myers, *The Story of the Three Kingdoms* (New York: HarperCollins, 1995).

16. Personal interview with Christopher Myers, March 18, 1998.

17. *Contemporary Authors*, (New Revision Series. 1995), p. 336.

FURTHER READING

Burshtein, Karen. *Walter Dean Myers*. New York: Rosen Publishing Group, 2003.

Marler, Myrna Dee. *Walter Dean Myers*. Westport, Conn.: Greenwood Press, 2008.

Mitchell, Susan Harkins. *Walter Dean Myers*. Hockessin, DE: Mitchell Lane Publishers, 2003

INTERNET ADDRESSES

Walter Dean Myers
The official website of Walter Dean Myers
<http://www.walterdeanmyers.net/>

Walter Dean Myers Biography
Provides a biography and interview transcript for Walter Dean Myers
<http://www.scholastic.com/teachers/contributor/walter-dean-myers>

INDEX